Remodelista

THE ORGANIZED HOME

Remodelista

THE ORGANIZED HOME

**Simple,
Stylish Storage
Ideas for
All Over
the House**

**Julie Carlson and
Margot Guralnick**

With the editors of REMODELISTA

Photographs by MATTHEW WILLIAMS
Creative direction by ALEXA HOTZ

ARTISAN | NEW YORK

Remodelista editor in chief Julie Carlson

Writer and producer Margot Guralnick

Photographer Matthew Williams

Creative direction Alexa Hotz

Co-producer Francesca Connolly

Resources Meredith Swinehart

Intern Alejandra Bennett

Library of Congress Cataloging-in-Publication Data

Names: Carlson, Julie, author. | Guralnick, Margot, author.
Title: Remodelista : the organized home / Julie Carlson and Margot Guralnick ; with the editors
   of Remodelista ; photographs by Matthew Williams ; creative direction by Alexa Hotz.
Other titles: Remodelista (2017)
Description: New York : Artisan, a division of Workman Publishing Co., Inc.
   [2017] | Includes index.
Identifiers: LCCN 2017013398 | ISBN 9781579656935 (paper-over-board)
Subjects: LCSH: Interior decoration—Themes, motives. | Orderliness. | Storage in the home.
Classification: LCC NK2115 .C275 2017 | DDC 648/.8—dc23 LC record available at https://lccn.
loc.gov/2017013398

Cover design by Michelle Ishay-Cohen
Cover photographs by Matthew Williams
Design by Rita Sowins / Sowins Design

Artisan books are available at special discounts when purchased in bulk for premiums and sales promotions as well as for fund-raising or educational use. Special editions or book excerpts also can be created to specification. For details, contact the Special Sales Director at the address below, or send an e-mail to specialmarkets@workman.com.

Published by Artisan
A division of Workman Publishing Co., Inc.
225 Varick Street
New York, NY 10014-4381
artisanbooks.com

Artisan is a registered trademark of Workman Publishing Co., Inc.

Published simultaneously in Canada by Thomas Allen & Son, Limited

Printed in China
First printing, October 2017

10 9 8 7 6 5 4 3 2 1

Contents

"For every minute spent in organizing, an hour is earned."

—BENJAMIN FRANKLIN

Introduction

Sometimes it seems you are what you own. We know that feeling. Like everyone, we aspire to sanity and order in our daily lives. But unlike most people, we devote our working hours to discovering and exploring inviting, serene homes. We here at Remodelista are a group of design-minded friends who make it our mission to decode all the details that go into well-put-together living quarters. And we strive to practice what we preach in our own homes, whether tiny studios or family houses, where we pare down, put away, and purchase thoughtfully—some days more successfully than others, but always with an invisible safety net of order.

We can help you achieve this clarity, too. With a little thought and effort, your home can become a place you look forward to returning to every day. It will feel not only more organized but also more spacious, lighter, and calmer. You will spend less time searching for misplaced keys and eyeglasses, and you won't need to hide so many things in drawers, because you'll love what you have.

Storage may be the underpinning of every uncluttered dwelling, but so much of what we've read on the subject is all about order over beauty. Our approach to solving organizational woes doesn't involve sacrificing style. We believe in focusing on the basics and celebrating the stuff of everyday life. We are advocates of the well-made and the utilitarian, such as straw baskets, canvas bins, and wooden peg rails. And we're all about arranging belongings in ways that aren't just tidy but also enhance your routine. Whether you're a minimalist or a collector, if you follow our lead, you'll have fewer but better things in your life and more moments of inspiration and satisfaction as you move through your day.

In this volume, we begin with the Remodelista organizational philosophy. Then, room by room, we present solutions for conquering the most challenging zones in your home—illustrated with hundreds of inspiring photographs by Matthew Williams, our talented collaborator. Along the way, we offer solutions to common blights, such as toilet brushes and snaking electrical cords, and share tips gleaned from innovative, organization-minded pros, from boat designers to kindergarten teachers. We conclude with our 75 favorite storage staples and a compendium of resources, including alternatives to household plastics and how to get rid of unwanted items of all sorts.

The result: easy-to-maintain spaces that are both orderly and artful, personal and purposeful. Because ultimately, the goal isn't a flawless, impossible-to-maintain showcase. The aim is an unencumbered life in a house that makes you happy.

The Art of Order: A Manifesto

We believe in better living through organization. Here are eight ways to get there.

01

Buy fewer (and better) things. Resist impulse and stopgap purchases. Instead, zero in on quality.

02

Donate the stuff you don't use. That includes unwanted gifts. Let someone else put your castoffs to good use.

03

Shop your own house. A surprising array of storage challenges can be solved with a well-made basket, tray, or hook—chances are, you already own most of the supplies that you need.

04

Steal ideas from organizational masters. Experts, such as hoteliers and shopkeepers, know how to come up with novel, affordable approaches to storage.

05

Ditch the plastic. Seek out products made of sustainable natural materials, such as wood, glass, and ceramic. They're better for the planet, and you won't have to stash them out of sight.

06

Know what you've got. Ample storage is not necessarily a good thing. We've been conditioned to think that huge closets are desirable, but the truth is, they can encourage you to avoid pruning your belongings (and to lose track of what you have).

07

Establish habits and routines that simplify your life: always keep your keys and eyeglasses in designated spots. (See "Daily Rituals," page 18, for more.)

08

Relax and make yourself at home. Too much enforced order is uninviting for occupants and guests alike; rooms are for living.

12 Universal Storage Tactics

You don't need cavernous closets and built-in cabinetry to have an orderly household. But you *do* need a place for everything. Here are our favorite organizational tricks to deploy all over the house. Look for them put into practice throughout the book.

TACTIC 01
Hang It

Lacking drawer space? Hooks, pegs, and peg rails are the answer for keeping things organized and handy. The beauty of this approach is threefold: these solutions often cost next to nothing, they're good-looking (even a nail has an honest charm), and they're easy to use, so everyone can be brought on board.

TACTIC 02
Cart It

From bar carts to industrial trolleys, there's a range of compact wheeled storage ideal for corralling collections of items in one place. Carts, of course, are easy to move, so they can be rolled out for use or tucked away as needed.

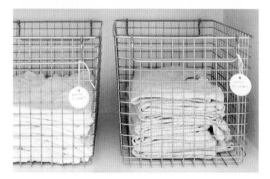

TACTIC 03
Label It

Name what you've got and you'll know what you've got—and where it goes. How else do you think a cockpit or an operating room functions? Use a Sharpie and tape (we like washi tape—made of rice paper—because it's removable). Or tie on stationery store tags. Sold on your label maker? Use it behind the scenes. For displayed goods, hand lettering is nicer to look at.

TACTIC 04
Tray It

Grouping objects on trays is the equivalent of adding frames to artwork: trays are the finishing touch that elevates what they contain and creates cohesion. Equally important, trays prevent things from getting lost: they provide a home for small, loose items of all sorts.

TACTIC 05
Shelve It

Strategically placed shelves are one of the great organizational building blocks. All it takes are simple hardware store parts to create shelving, so plant a ledge wherever you can use one. For a list of ready-made shelving systems that we swear by, see page 210.

TACTIC 06
Stack It

Kitchen tableware is made to stack. Books and magazines also stack well, both vertically and horizontally. So does firewood. And there's a world of stacking furniture worth seeking out (like the Frosta stools from Ikea pictured above). Stacking is about using space efficiently, but stick to small numbers of items: you don't want to live surrounded by Jenga towers.

TACTIC 07
Door It

Like walls, doors can be used to hold hooks and all manner of purpose-built shelves and racks (the over-the-door metal hook above is by Yamazaki; the Container Store's Elfa system also has good door-mounted options for pantry goods, entryway accessories, and more). Unlike walls, doors have two sides, so these solutions needn't be in full view. A word of advice: resist outfitting every door; the goal is to create a few jangle-free spots in which to keep your most-used things.

TACTIC 08
Wrangle It

A web of visible electrical cords is one of the biggest eyesores in a house. Tackle the situation like a gardener ousting weeds: take both gentle and, as needed, desperate measures. A simple metal binder clip curbs unruliness (see above), as does installing strategically placed electrical outlets all over, including on the floor near the sofa and in the back of bathroom drawers. Hide cords and routers in boxes. And use storage space to keep as much of the tangle as possible out of sight.

TACTIC 09
Decant It

Stop the encroachment of unappealing, bulky packaging the way chefs and scientists do. New to decanting? Start in the kitchen by storing your olive oil, hand soap, and other liquids in pretty bottles and grains and pastas in canning jars. Not only will you gain shelf space, but you'll also be able to see what you've got, and it will line up seamlessly. Then employ this strategy all over the house, for everything from paper clips to Legos.

TACTIC 10
Kit It

Just about all of us have kits for certain everyday essentials: tools, first-aid supplies, sewing paraphernalia. Whether in a drawer, box, or other container, keeping related pieces in established places is a boon. So we've discovered that it makes good sense to assemble more kits for whatever it is you regularly need to do: pack a suitcase, send out a batch of thank-you notes, or throw an impromptu dinner party. You'll discover our kits in every room in the book.

TACTIC 11
Sort It

Group like with like and use matching
storage items: uniformity telegraphs
cohesion. Lining up identical things, such
as wooden hangers (white for shirts, natural
for pants), wire baskets, and cardboard
binders, is a trick used by architects and
designers to create a look of order.

TACTIC 12
Repurpose It

Think outside the box when it comes to
storage items: a magazine file mounted
inside a cabinet door is exactly the
right size for a lineup of kitchen wrap
(see above); covered enamel kitchen
containers make excellent bins for cotton
balls, swabs, and other essentials. When
objects are made with care, it shows—and
they can be put to use just about anywhere.

Daily Rituals

For a sense of calm and control, these are the seven simple habits that we swear by. You should, too: they collectively take no more than a few minutes of effort each day, and they're life-changing.

01

Make your bed every morning. Opt for a seasonal duvet with a cotton or linen cover (in lieu of a flat sheet) and this becomes a fifteen-second feat. Studies have shown that bed makers are not only more rested than non–bed makers but also happier, healthier, and more successful.

02

Hang up your coat on arrival; resist the urge to drape it on the nearest surface.

03

Keep your keys in a designated spot. (For easy solutions, go to page 30.)

04

Tuck a lightweight market tote in your bag when you leave the house to avoid bringing home a stream of paper and plastic shopping bags.

05

Open mail daily. Then toss or file.

06

Do a quick clean sweep before turning in at night. Wipe the kitchen counters, hang backpacks, and gather stray shoes in a basket. Bonus points: establish a charging station (see page 38) and religiously plug in your electronics at night. It's nice to start the day at 100 percent.

07

Put away your clothes at bedtime: hang, fold, or toss in a laundry hamper. If you're given to piling clothes on the floor or a chair, wall hooks are the answer.

The
Entry

way

A clean entry is essential; no one wants to open the door to a mess. Make the effort to establish a well-thought-out entrance and it will change the course of your day—no more mornings spent on the hunt for errant objects. There are blessedly few requirements: keep your by-the-door items to a minimum, leave room to maneuver, and don't treat this area as a dumping ground. What can't be hung or stowed in a drawer or basket doesn't belong. Once you've established a system, train yourself and the people you live with to use it: on arrival, always, always put your keys, coats, and bags in their assigned spots. It's that simple.

4

A Shaker-Style Entry

A storage-lined open foyer is a great, versatile option for busy households. This one employs several items in "The Remodelista Storage 75" (beginning on page 162) and takes inspiration from the Shaker use of peg rails to hang all manner of things. To assemble your own version, all you need is a sliver of hall off your front or back door. Here's why this setup works.

1 **Pegs close to the entrance** help ensure that kids' bags land in the right spot. (Parents' bags go on the other end.)

2 **A peg rail** can also be used as a picture rail.

3 **Designated coat pegs** offer a spot for each family member.

4 **A Shaker-style hanging shelf from Pottery Barn** provides a home for small items, including sunblock in a basket, keys, and a sunglasses tray.

5 **A chalkboard** is used to mark daily reminders and important details, such as telephone numbers for babysitters to know.

6 **A canvas tote** holds current favorite scarves and caps.

7 **An Ikea Tjusig bench** doubles as a shoe rack; it has room for ten pairs.

8 **A bentwood tray** is the landing spot for the daily mail.

The Entryway

STEAL THIS LOOK

A Hardworking Family Mudroom

This well-planned urban entry—designed by architect Annabelle Selldorf for a family of four—has a place for everything, from balls to backpacks and more. Here's why it works.

1 **Labeled canvas bins** hold the daily essentials. There's a bin for each member of the family, plus designated bins for hats, helmets, and shopping bags.

2 **Cubbies** surround a long coat rail, offering multiple storage opportunities.

3 **A canvas tote** slung over a coat hanger creates a place to stash rackets.

4 **A Japanese circular hanger** provides a pretty way to store scarves.

5 **An indoor doormat,** a companion to one outside, helps keep dirt from being tracked in.

6 **A repurposed jelly-roll pan** serves as a boot tray.

STEAL THIS LOOK

A Versatile Apartment-Sized Entry

For tight quarters and setups that lack a foyer, it's easy to create your own entryway—especially if you begin with a freestanding design that covers the main bases. Bonus: this tidy ensemble can come with you if you move. Here's why it works.

1 **A wall-mounted entry unit** offers places to hang as well as stow essentials. This Remodelista favorite is from Stattmann Neue Moebel in Germany (Crate & Barrel and Ikea both also sell good options).

2 **A high shelf** gathers hats and tote bags.

3 **Pegs** serve as hanging places not just for coats but also for a dog leash, a leather key fob, and a portable light by Flos.

4 **A small alarm clock** helps keep proceedings on task.

5 **A hanging mirror** stands at the ready for that quick check before you head out the door.

6 **Divided compartments** contain zones for mail, keys, and loose change.

7 **A stool** provides a perch for putting on and taking off shoes, and for reaching the top shelf. This one is an eBay purchase upgraded with Farrow & Ball gray paint.

8 **A sturdy basket** is a place to toss shoes on arrival.

9 **A Muji umbrella bin** works well as a yoga-mat holder.

The Secret to a Streamlined Entry

A little bit of daily maintenance goes a long way here, beginning with managing the mail. Digitize what you can. For the rest, pick a place to put the day's mail (see page 31 for some good solutions) and make a habit of going through it immediately, pitching what you don't need and distributing the rest (consider establishing containers for personal correspondence, bills, magazines, and things to file). Then build in a seasonal deep clean following the guidelines below.

What to Toss

- Broken umbrellas

- Keys to nowhere

- Orphaned gloves

- Outgrown kids' wear

- Unused sports equipment and past-their-prime tennis balls

- Junk mail

- Unnecessary multiples of anything

- Excess shoes and bags (the entry is only for those you use daily; relocate all others—and get rid of old favorites that have expired)

- Out-of-season outerwear (unless you have a big closet that leaves room for guest coats, put bulky winter items into storage elsewhere in the house)

For good ways to unload unwanted things, see pages 194–198.

Where to Keep Your Keys

Pick an option that works for you: hang, stow, or toss in a set spot.
What matters is that you find a system and scrupulously stick with it.
Here are four strategies we like.

Cup Hooks

Color-Coded Hooks

Magnetic Knife Rack

Tray or Bowl

Where to Keep Your Mail

Incoming and outgoing letters can get lost in the shuffle, unless there's one place they belong. Designate a landing zone and you'll be able to keep track of important mail and guard against pileups.

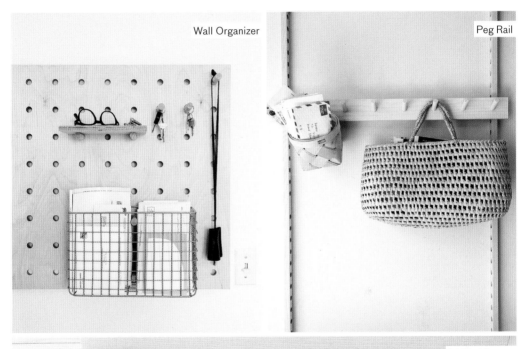

Wall Organizer

Peg Rail

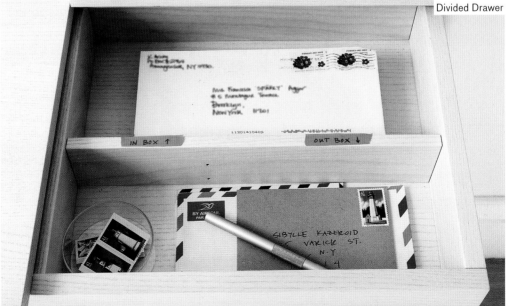

Divided Drawer

Think Like a Shaker

The Shakers were the original minimalists. The egalitarian religious sect believed that living simply was a sacred calling and that cleanliness was godliness. We are continually inspired by their pared-down approach to design, which is all about smart storage. Here are five Shaker ideas to apply to your home from **Lesley Herzberg**, curator of Hancock Shaker Village in Pittsfield, Massachusetts.

1 **Discover the power of the peg rail.** The Shakers wrapped whole rooms in these humble storage devices, deploying them both high and low, and often in double rows. The point, says Herzberg: "to make tidiness automatic."

2 **Hang more than just clothes.** Anything with a loop on it can be suspended from a peg: in the entryway pictured opposite, a shoehorn, mirror, key holder, and Stanley Ruiz maple clock are neatly arrayed.

3 **Love your broom.** When the utilitarian is beautiful, it becomes decorative.

4 **Choose furniture that's easy to move.** This allows for adaptable spaces and simplifies floor cleaning. The Shaker signature slat-rail chair is intentionally light: when not in use, it can be hung on pegs (upside down to keep dust from settling on seats).

5 **Look within.** Cupboards and bureaus are space hogs, but not if they're built in. The Shakers turned the spaces between structural supports in their walls into drawers, shelves, and cabinets. Knock on walls with a carpenter and discover your own hidden storage world.

Where to Corral the Footwear

We're proponents of shoe removal on arrival: It keeps the floors and hence the whole house cleaner. Here are some simple shoe storage options for the entry.

Metal Tray

Good for a few favorite pairs of shoes, and essential for muddy and wet gear. This one from Crate & Barrel is made of galvanized iron and has a doormat-like nubby rubber liner. (We also like jelly roll pans borrowed from the kitchen.)

Storage Bench

Just about all entries could use one of these: a place to sit *and* stow your things. This limited-edition Ikea bench is one you could make yourself if you're handy. The lid opens to reveal a trio of labeled Korbo baskets for slippers, shoes, and sneakers.

Cubbies

An idea borrowed from the kindergarten classroom: segmented shelves with spots for everyone in the house. They're available from the Container Store, among other sources.

Baskets and Bins

A selling point of baskets is that they're portable, and a French market tote adds a touch of Gallic style. Wooden crates also work well.

PREPAREDNESS KIT

The Elevated Junk Drawer

Create a utility drawer in your entry or kitchen for toolbox basics
(items you reach for on a regular basis). Having this central supply
station saves you a trip to the basement, garage, or shed, and in case
of a blackout, you're prepared.

The Essentials

- Utility scissors
- Flashlight
- Hammer and nails
- Pliers
- Screwdriver
- Wrench
- Box cutter
- Batteries
- Masking tape
- Measuring tape
- Pushpins
- String or twine
- Rubber bands

Also Consider

- Candles and matches
- Picture wire
- Jar for pocket change
- Magnifying glass

The Electronics Charging Station

Keep your digital gear at the ready and combat cord creep by inserting concealed charging stations wherever they'll come in handy. Shown here are two good, out-of-sight places to park electronics: a divided drawer in an entryway (opposite) and a pullout desk at the end of a kitchen cabinet (below).

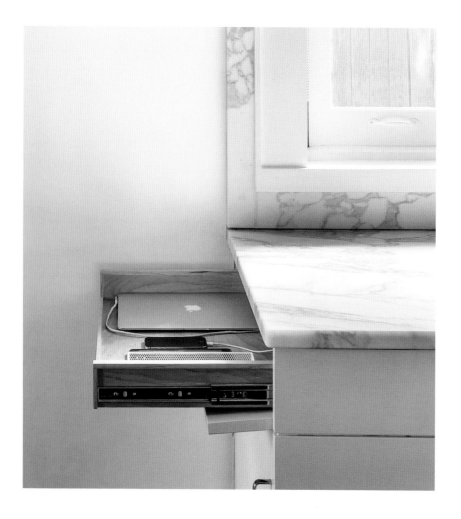

Think Like a Kindergarten Teacher

If untamed five-year-olds can be taught to put their things away, so can you and your family. Here, **Howard Garrett**, a kindergarten teacher at Saint Ann's School in Brooklyn, New York, summarizes seven classroom tools and tactics that translate well at home.

1 **Choose storage that's accessible, visible, and portable, such as cubbies and containers.** When it's obvious where things go, they're much more likely to land in the right spots.

2 **Label everything.** Use words or even simple drawings—or both—to underscore your system. No need to get fancy with your labels: block lettering does the trick.

3 **Establish storage zones.** Group items throughout your home by theme: a place for coats, bags, and keys when you walk in the door; ample bookshelves for filing reading material; a cupboard, closet, or wall for the broom and other utility supplies.

4 **Limit the number of objects you take out at one time**—and put them away before moving on to the next activity. This reduces the mess and makes cleanup much less overwhelming.

5 **Spell out tasks and incentives.** Everyone needs to understand the daily responsibilities and rewards.

6 **Make cleanup fun.** Turn up the volume on your sound system while you work.

7 **Lay on the praise.** It takes patience and Pavlovian tactics for tidying to become habitual: you'll be much more effective if rather than ranting about sloppiness you single out good behavior. Kind words and compliments are the answer.

The
Kitch

en

We demand a lot of our kitchens: our most lived-in room is expected to be a high-functioning cooking station *plus* an intimate hangout space. Whatever their size or look, most kitchens, we've discovered, are many pounds overweight with unnecessary cooking gear, tableware, and canned and dry goods. You can lose this excess with ease and gain maneuverability and livability. Read our list of what you really need and then devote an afternoon to a kitchen edit (see pages 50–51). As you organize, take a look at our kitchen storage solutions and borrow as many as you can.

The Ultimate Compact Kitchen

This small workspace makes good use of open and closed storage: cookware and dishware are concealed behind cabinet doors, and a clever storage rail keeps often-used tools close at hand but off the counter. The design also employs just about every one of our universal storage tactics (see pages 12–17). And it's plastic-free (find our list of alternatives to plastic on pages 192–193). Here's why it works.

1 **Stacked dishware and decanted pantry goods** maximize cabinet space.

2 **An Ikea Dignitet curtain rod wire** acts as a hanging rail for essentials.

3 **S hooks and metal clips** keep, among other things, kitchen scissors, coffee filters, and a dish scrubber on hand.

4 **Trays** anchor the counter: an enameled tray corrals dishwashing essentials, and a jelly-roll pan serves as a dish drainer base.

5 **A Hugo Guinness print** adds an artful touch— a small detail that makes a big difference. Why shouldn't you display art in the kitchen?

6 **A small hanging basket** holds the vegetable peeler and other tools.

7 **Stainless steel containers** nest and are an environmentally friendly food storage option.

EXPERT ADVICE

Think Like a Chef

In a professional kitchen, tools need to be grabbable, but work counters have to be kept clear—and space is almost always at a premium. So whom better to look to for culinary storage tricks than **Dana Cowin,** former longtime editor in chief of *Food & Wine*? Here are her top five tips learned on the job.

1 **Adhere to the French notion of *mise en place* (everything in its place).** In a chef's kitchen, the spoons never migrate. The pans are always where they were the last time you used them. "Think Julia Child and her pegboard for pots," says Cowin.

2 **Keep everything visible and within arm's reach.** Hang pots and pans from S hooks, suspend utensils from a rail, and store knives in a rack (so they don't overlap and become dull). According to Cowin, "Chefs would abolish most drawers if they could."

3 **Pare down.** Because of cost and space, chefs confine themselves to only the most necessary equipment (see "Take a Kitchen Inventory—and Shed the Excess," pages 50–51).

4 **Buy staples in bulk and repackage them in smaller, easy-to-store tubs.** Yes, even chefs advocate decanting, especially for ingredients like flour, sugar, and cornmeal. No lugging required: in their new containers, these staples should be lined up and readily accessible, whether on a shelf or in a drawer.

5 **Shop at restaurant supply stores.** These are great places to buy things for the home, such as cutting boards, white plates, and stainless steel pot racks. The goods are well priced and made for heavy use. (For a list of sources and items to zero in on, see page 216.)

The Kitchen

In Praise of Trays

Trays are handy throughout the house, but our all-time favorite use for them is as a home base for sink-side and stove-side essentials. The appeal ranges from the practical (trays are portable and easy to clean) to the aesthetic (grouped as an ensemble, humble tools on a tray become a Giorgio Morandi–esque still life). Note that there's no need to stop at just one: trays within trays create visual order and make it easy to organize small items.

Take a Kitchen Inventory— and Shed the Excess

Here's what we consider the bare minimum essentials, plus ideas for what to deaccession.

What You Need

Prepware

- 3 knives: a chef's knife, a paring knife, and a serrated knife
- 2 cutting boards (1 for vegetables, 1 for meat)
- Vegetable peeler
- Box grater
- Microplane
- Kitchen shears
- Can opener
- Colander
- Wooden spoon
- Spatula
- Whisk
- Pair of tongs
- Meat thermometer

Cookware

- 8-quart covered saucepan
- 14-quart covered pasta pot
- 8- to 10-inch cast-iron pan
- 14-inch skillet
- Dutch oven

Bakeware

- 2 sets of measuring cups (one for liquids and another for dry goods, such as flour and sugar)
- Set of measuring spoons
- 3 mixing bowls in graduated sizes (choose a set that also works for serving food and storing leftovers)
- Rimmed baking sheet
- Trio of cake pans

Tableware

- 2 dinner- and lunch-size plates, cereal bowls, drinking glasses, and sets of flatware per family member, plus 2 to 4 extra sets for guests (depending on how often you entertain)
- 2 serving platters

Other Equipment

- 2 pot holders or oven mitts
- 4 kitchen towels
- Storage containers
- Blender and/or food processor
- Coffeemaker

What to Toss

- **Unnecessary gadgets and accessories.** How often do you use that panini press? How about all those extra cutting boards? And is that cherry pitter something you get out more than once a year?

- **Excess dishes.** See "Tableware" (opposite) for our rule of thumb: you need daily dinnerware for only twice the number of people in your household.

- **Sets of everyday** *and* **formal dishware.** Stick with one neutral design that you love. We like all white: it comes in a huge variety of options, both refined and rustic, and you can dress it up or down with other table accessories, such as place mats, cloth napkins, and greenery.

- **Mismatched tableware.** Sets stack best; lone plates, bowls, and mugs should be weeded out—or at least whittled down to one or two favorites.

- **Space-hogging appliances that you rarely use.** Move out all but the daily essentials; if you bake only on occasion, for instance, consider storing the mixer elsewhere.

- **Unloved gifts.** Give yourself permission to deaccession the odd set of four dessert plates, the crystal vase, the decorative bowl. Kitchen storage is too precious for the unused.

- **Expired spices and canned goods.** Check the "use by" dates and toss anything that doesn't make the cut. Going forward, avoid the waste by keeping fewer things on hand: those cans in the back are unlikely to ever become dinner. Same goes for hidden pantry goods such as grains and pastas.

For good ways to unload unwanted things, see pages 194–198.

Cookware Storage: Easy Access Is the Answer

Lend order to your cabinets by wrangling your pots and pans. Reaching your favorites should not require excavational skills.

Hang

Use S hooks to suspend pots and pans from a utensil rail. In this narrow galley kitchen, a steel pipe makes efficient use of the wall space between counter and shelf.

Nest

The answer for multiples of anything large or heavy is to use matched sets that fit together (like these Revol porcelain baking dishes). Nesting allows you to store multiples in a single footprint.

Stack

Add dish risers to a pullout shelf to create tiers for pots, heavy casserole dishes, and bakeware. You'll be able to fit more in a small space.

Shelve

A custom-fitted corner cupboard, such as this example by top German kitchen company Bulthaup, makes use of otherwise hard-to-reach space. An inexpensive ready-made option is to fit your corner cupboard with a large wooden lazy Susan.

The Kitchen

Pot Lid Storage:
Separate and Stash

Lids tend to get lost in the shuffle. Give them a place to belong—
grouped together—and you'll always know where they are.

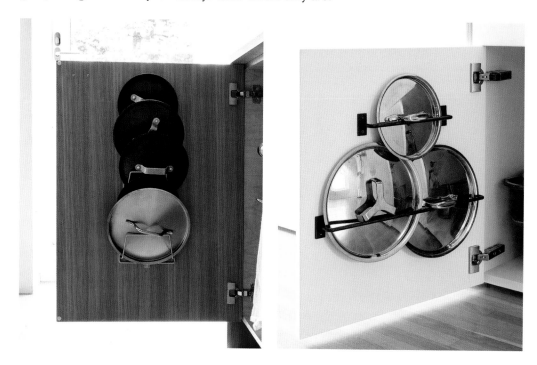

Put Your Doors to Work

In an architect-designed kitchen, a metal pot lid rack mounted on the
inside of a cabinet door (above left) offers a pot-lid storage solution. Our
DIY version (above right) puts Japanese metal towel rods to the same use.

Buy the Right Tools

A deep drawer nicely accommodates a metal lid rack from Ikea that works like an office paper sorter.

Pen Them In

A hardware store tension rod inserted at the very front of a drawer keeps pot lids neatly in place.

The Kitchen

Knife Storage: On Hand and In Order

Throwing knives together in a drawer can lead to dull blades. Here are some good ways to keep your tools sharp and at close range.

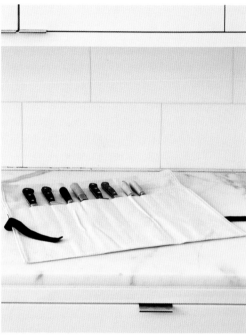

Chef's Rack

Made from lightweight stainless steel, a wall-hung knife holder is an inexpensive fixture at restaurant supply stores. This one cost ten dollars and has slots that accommodate five knives plus a sharpening steel.

Canvas Case

Chefs travel with their knives in roll-up leather and canvas cases. This one from English cutlery specialist David Mellor has twelve compartments and can be wound into a compact bundle for storage in a drawer or on the go.

Magnetic Rack

Hang knives and scissors by their blades on magnetic strips and they'll always be ready and waiting. This rack by Jacob May for Quitokeeto is especially nice because it's made of bleached maple (with concealed magnets) and comes with brass hardware. (Magnetic racks also work as key holders—see page 30.)

Knife Block

Store your tools alongside your cutting board in a compact block. This plywood design by David Mellor is a modern take on a classic.

The Kitchen

Think Like a Shopkeeper

In retail parlance, it's called *merchandising*: the art of arranging goods so that they're easy to access and visually appealing. Here are six principles from **Sam Hamilton**, kitchen designer and owner of San Francisco couture kitchen boutique March. Apply them to your kitchen and you'll have much more "shoppable" space.

1 **Use shallow pantry storage.** The items that are visible are the ones you'll use (just as with the retail mantra "What you can see is what sells"). So line your goods up front and make use of risers in the back. When installing storage, measure accordingly: "You don't want shelves that hold more than two rows of cans," advises Hamilton. "Anything deeper and things get lost in the void."

2 **Create kitchen zones.** Just as retailers group goods by theme, you should set up areas in your kitchen for coffeemaking, food prep, and so on. Cluster culinary essentials on trays to anchor them.

3 **Consider proximity.** Daily dishware belongs on the shelves closest to your sink and dishwasher, for ease of loading and unloading.

4 **Leave yourself elbow room at the sink.** Keep your work area as clear as a checkout counter. Ask yourself, "What do I use here all the time?" Relocate the rest.

5 **Conquer drawer space by dividing it.** Size up what you're stowing and create compartments accordingly, so that nothing is free-floating or jumbled. You can buy ready-made drawer inserts from places like Ikea and the Container Store.

6 **Look up, look down.** In stores, plenty of inventory is kept on hand but out of sight. The same rule applies in kitchens: deep corner cabinets work well as appliance garages. And high cabinets are ideal for storing occasionally used tableware. For access to these spots, keep a step stool or a rolling ladder handy.

Dish and Glassware Storage: Beyond the Kitchen Cabinet

Tableware that gets used every day should be stored front and center: aim for a spot as close to the sink and dishwasher as possible.

On the Wall

Much like the compact shelves made for ship galleys, this Indian stainless steel classic (sourced online from Stovold & Pogue) does double duty: it serves as both a drying and storage rack. And if one rack doesn't hold enough for your household, add another—but embrace the enforced minimalism of the design.

In a Cart

An industrial metal cart holds a lot of tableware—and can be wheeled directly to the table for setting. This example, filled with creamware pitchers, mixing bowls, and platters, belongs to London chef, shop owner, and bon vivant Alastair Hendy.

On Open Shelves

Shelves stocked with glassware are especially convenient when positioned over the sink. Designed by architect Elizabeth Roberts, this tiny kitchen has a restaurant supply store stainless steel counter and custom overhead storage.

In a Drawer

Glassware doesn't have to live above the counter. A deep drawer can make it more accessible for all, and easier to fill from the adjacent dishwasher.

The Kitchen

The Instant Cocktail Party

You're more likely to throw an impromptu drinks or dinner party when your tabletop elements are kept at the ready in one place. A kitchen or dining area drawer is especially handy for this kit. Pro tip: store the items on trays so you can lift them out for quick delivery to the table—and then use the trays for serving.

The Essentials

- Bar tools: corkscrew, bottle opener, jigger, and mixing spoon

- Candles: tapers and tea lights

- Matches

- Ice bucket

- Glasses

- Serving trays

Also Consider

- Ready-for-the-table flatware sets in leather pockets (see page 65 for more information.)

- Cloth napkins rolled in napkin rings

Flatware Storage: Beyond the Utensil Drawer

Cutlery trays are exemplars of order, but improvised systems can be equally winning. Consider your setup and pick the best approach for you.

The New Silverware Chest

An idea spotted at Cosme, in New York: Bisley office supply drawers used on a sideboard or tabletop to stow forks, knives, and spoons. Like the concept? Learn about this mini cabinet in "The Remodelista Storage 75," page 174.

A High-Edged Tray

This ceramic design neatly holds flatware for eight—and stands ready to be moved from counter to table.

Open Containers

Another option when drawer space is at a premium: consider sorting everyday flatware into a trio of metal or ceramic canisters. These are 28-ounce tomato cans with the paper labels removed; they rest on trays from Fog Linen (one of the designs included in "The Remodelista Storage 75"; see page 187).

Ready-to-Go Flatware Pockets

Pouches sized for a fork, spoon, and knife make setting the table a fait accompli. Our leather examples are a collaboration between March of San Francisco and RTH of Los Angeles. You can also stitch your own out of cloth napkins or heavy fabric.

The Kitchen

Where to Put the Paper Towels

While we're all trying to cut down on our use of paper towels, they remain a presence in most kitchens. Here are some out-of-sight places to stow them.

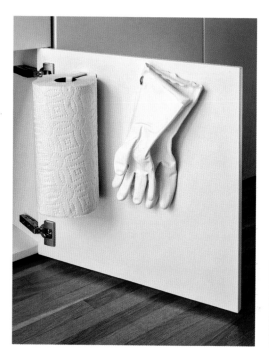

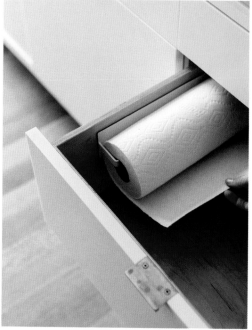

On a Cabinet Door

Open the cabinet under your kitchen sink and you'll discover unused territory: a metal paper towel holder (this one is made by Yamazaki) fits neatly on the inside. There's also room to install a hook for another staple, dishwashing gloves.

In a Drawer

Stow your paper towels in a drawer by affixing a metal paper towel holder, like this one from Yamazaki, on an interior surface, where it's hidden but accessible.

In a Cupboard

Paper towels can be dispensed via a spring-loaded, adjustable tension rod from the hardware store.

In a Cabinet

A pair of adjustable metal drapery rod brackets (these are from Umbra) and a hardware store wooden dowel create a good, simple way to hang a paper towel roll. And it needn't be out in the open: this one is mounted in a cabinet under the sink.

Decant and Corral Your Way to an Organized Pantry

A jumble of packaging—outsized boxes of cereal, sacks of flour and sugar, and plastic bags of dried beans and pasta—makes it impossible to use your cabinets efficiently. Take a moment to decant your pantry essentials before loading them onto shelves (buy in bulk when possible) and you'll gain space, order, and a much prettier overall picture.

Designer Michaela Scherrer created open storage in her kitchen (opposite) by simply removing old cabinet doors that she didn't like. A decanting devotee, she stocks her shelves with a harmonious mix of Weck glass canning jars for dry goods, stacked tins for herbs and spices, and collaged cardboard boxes that she fills with tea.

PREPAREDNESS KIT

The Herb and Spice Drawer

Create a designated place for herbs and frequently used tools like a garlic press and graters. Dried herbs have a short shelf life, especially if they're exposed to light, so keeping only small quantities makes sense, as does arranging them in a drawer or cupboard. No fitted insert necessary; corral everything on trays. Here's what you need.

The Essentials

- Uniform glass jars— we like small paint jars from the art supply store (see "The Remodelista Storage 75," page 179)

- Metal trays sized to fit your drawer

- Washi tape for labeling the jar tops (this is an idea we like from cookbook author Heidi Swanson)

Also Consider

- Herb scissors

- Spice grinder

- Garlic press

- Ginger grater

- Small bowls for specialty salts

PREPAREDNESS KIT

The Plastic-Free Pantry and Fridge

Our quest to rid our lives of plastic extends to food storage—and there are plenty of scientific studies to back us up on this one. We recommend replacing that Tupperware with tried-and-true storage staples made of natural materials. Find sourcing details in "The Remodelista Storage 75," pages 179–183, and more ideas in "Alternatives to Plastic," pages 192–193. And learn daily tactics from zero-waste-living advocates; we take inspiration from Bea Johnson of ZeroWasteHome.com and Lauren Singer of TrashIsforTossers.com.

The Essentials

- Cotton produce bags

- Glass canning jars and enamelware canisters

- Metal clips

- Washi tape and a marker

- Bee's Wrap and other natural alternatives to plastic wrap

Also Consider

- Linen bowl covers

- Paper bags (good for keeping mushrooms fresh in the produce drawer)

- Furoshiki cloth (see page 182)

Think Like a Foodie

Good cooks care about the way kitchen staples are stored. How to tame the jungle inside our refrigerators? **Karen Mordechai,** food photographer, founder of Sunday Suppers, and cookbook author, has six smart answers.

1 **Buy in smaller quantities and avoid overcrowding.** "I've learned over the years to purchase food in a more thoughtful manner," says Mordechai. "Sometimes that means shopping more frequently, but I'm okay with that. I love having a refrigerator that feels approachable and inspiring."

2 **Establish distinct storage zones.** To avoid a free-for-all, store like with like to introduce predictability and order. In most fridges, the bottom shelf is the coldest zone, making it ideal for meat; beverages do well on the top shelf; vinegar-based condiments (such as ketchup and mustard) belong in the door compartments, which are less chilly. Leftovers, meanwhile, should be clustered at eye level where they're sure to be noticed.

3 **Practice first in, first out.** Adopted from grocers and other retailers, the FIFO approach ensures that what needs to be used first, such as milk that will soon expire, is stocked up front.

4 **Commit to a once-a-week fridge cleanup and clear-out.** "I find this very therapeutic," says Mordechai. "It always inspires a kitchen-sink meal or two, such as a frittata, a soup, and a big salad."

5 **Use enamel, ceramic, and glass containers.** Unlike plastic, they can go directly from fridge to oven to table (and your food doesn't have to mingle with things like BPA and phthalates). Label containers with washi tape to keep track of contents and dates.

6 **Store produce in reusable cloth and mesh bags (instead of plastic).** For sources, see page 182. And use your fridge properly: The high-humidity drawer is for things that wilt, such as greens, herbs, and strawberries. Oranges, apples, stone fruits, avocados, and other ethylene producers go in the low-humidity drawer.

The Bathr

oom

Clean and uncluttered is the impression you want from a bathroom. And since storage is at a premium in just about all bathrooms, every counter, drawer, and cabinet is prime real estate. Here is a series of easy-to-replicate bathroom solutions, all of which make use of practical—and presentable—receptacles gathered from around the house, especially the kitchen (see page 86).

A Well-Organized Console Sink

How to achieve inner beauty in a bathroom cabinet? Weed out the excess, gather small items in storage containers, and establish a hierarchy, so that what you use most is up front. Here's why this console works.

1 **Small trays** corral counter essentials.

2 **A touch of nature** brightens the whole sink top.

3 **Enamelware kitchen canisters** camouflage toiletries, such as dental floss and cotton balls.

4 **A portable tool caddy** holds cleaning supplies.

5 **A zippered toiletry kit** contains medicine cabinet overflow.

6 **A canvas bucket** stows extra TP.

7 **A wire basket** keeps hand towels and washcloths tidily folded and easy to spot.

STEAL THIS LOOK

The Medicine Cabinet as Vanity

We all long for a bathroom that feels like a spa. Unattainable in a small bath? Not entirely: you can create your own moment of Zen beauty in your medicine cabinet. All you have to do is remove the pileup of unused things and medicine bottles (in fact, it's actually better to store medicine at room temperature and away from moisture). Instead, devote the cabinet to your grooming arsenal: makeup, perfume, even jewelry. And whenever you open the cabinet, it will make you happy. Here's why this one works.

1 **An outlet on the inside of the cabinet** is ideal for electric toothbrushes, razors, and hair dryers.

2 **Shelves organized according to purpose:** beauty products on one shelf, skin care items on another, and dental care items on the easiest-to-access bottom tier.

3 **No excess**—and no searching required; what's here is a distillation of favorites.

4 **A variety of pretty vessels,** such as labware-style glass containers and a vintage silver cup, ensure that nothing is loose or untethered.

5 **A travel clock** keeps you on schedule.

6 **Vetiver root bundles** (from Bell'Occhio) offer a surprise hint of fragrance every time you open the cabinet.

7 **An over-the-door metal rack** (by Yamazaki) puts the inside of the mirror to good use as hanging jewelry storage.

7 Things to Get Rid of in the Bathroom

1 The toiletries/makeup you use less than once a week.

2 Expired medications and cosmetics.

3 Hotel-size items (if you like them for travel, keep them in your travel kit; see page 116).

4 More than one tube of toothpaste, comb and brush, nail clipper, pair of tweezers, bottle of aspirin, etc. (As for the things you swear by, such as your favorite conditioner and moisturizer, we subscribe to the Rule of Two: don't keep more than one backup—and, if possible, store it in a closet outside the bathroom.)

5 Unloved perfume.

6 Rusty disposable razors (consider replacing them with a refillable model).

7 Used-up nail polish, worn-out emery boards, soap slivers, and other spent goods.

And While We're on the Topic . . . How Many Towels Should You Own?

We know of space-challenged households that keep only one bath towel per person (plus an extra for a guest) and two hand towels (one hangs in the shared bath and gets changed midweek). That sounds reasonable to us, but in reality we stock at least two bath towels and hand towels per family member, along with plenty of washcloths.

Use Display-Worthy Vessels and Containers in the Bath

Browse your own house to find receptacles that fit your bathroom storage needs. See the following pages for more ideas.

1 An undivided drawer ends up being an undifferentiated mess. Partition your things on trays or in boxes or other containers. We're partial to these white enamelware basics from, among other places, art supply stores (they're sold as paint palettes). Leave space around objects, so you can see what you've got— and so what you've got is pretty to behold.

2 There's no getting around it: there are certain household goods that are nice to have on hand but aren't great to look at. When decanting isn't an option, consider camouflage—a bottle of Ibuprofen fits neatly inside a covered ceramic canister.

3 Create new uses for familiar things: a small woven basket holds an electric razor, and a pretty drinking glass is a great place to stash your eyeglasses.

4 A slim ceramic vase is perfect for a tube of toothpaste, a ceramic cup holds toothbrushes, and a clear glass container (see "The Remodelista Storage 75," page 181) is sized right for dental floss.

Kitchen Storage Solutions Can Work Well in the Bath . . .

Well-made, utilitarian storage should be deployed all over the house. So share the good ideas by repurposing the following items.

- Covered glass and enamelware food containers for toiletries

- Small metal trays as drawer dividers and countertop corrals

- Drinking glasses as eyeglass, toothpaste, and makeup-brush holders

- Lazy Susans as under-the-sink cabinet organizers

... and Vice Versa

- Wall-mounted soap dishes as kitchen brush and sponge holders
- Bathroom towel bars as dishcloth holders
- Medicine cabinets as herb and spice cabinets
- Soap on a rope as kitchen sink hand soap

1

2

3

4

Maximize Your Verticals

Even compact bathrooms have unused space perfect for stowing your shower basics, extra towels, jewelry, and more. It's all a matter of getting the hang of it.

1 S hooks turn a towel rod into a place for not only towels but also for other bathroom necessities.

2 No room for extra towels? Gather them, rolled, in a deep bag and suspend from a sink-side hook.

3 Mount a small kitchen rail on a wall as a place for a hand towel.

4 An S hook on a metal shampoo shelf is perfect for hanging a washcloth and soap on a rope (an old favorite that's been making a comeback; we love it because it air-dries).

Stowing the Unmentionables

Even the lowliest basics in the bathroom can be put on display, and you needn't look far for good storage options. Here are some simple examples.

Where to Put the Extra TP

Break the habit of ripping open a pack of toilet paper and propping the plastic-encased extras in full view. Instead, remove the packaging and pick an attractive storage container, such as a small woven basket (above left) or a metal breadbox (above right) for backup rolls.

Where to Put the Toilet Brush

A toilet-cleaning kit needn't be cringeworthy. Choose a non-plastic brush, like this Iris Hantverk birch-handled option with easy-to-clean bristles (available from Amazon, among other sources), and stow it in a pleasing container such as a terra-cotta planter complete with a handy drain and saucer (above left) or an Ikea enamelware pitcher resting on a Fog Linen tray (above right).

The Bathroom

Where to Put the Blow-Dryer

Take a tip from hoteliers: give your blow-dryer a spot to belong that keeps it handy but out of sight.

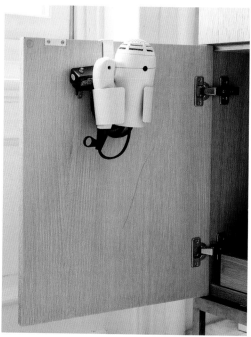

In a Drawer

Add an outlet to the back of a drawer and you've created the perfect place to store a blow-dryer anchored on a tray. (Similarly, if you add an outlet to a medicine cabinet, you have an ideal setup for an electric toothbrush.)

On a Cabinet Door

A holster inside a cabinet puts unused space to work. This hanging metal design is by Yamazaki.

In a Canvas Bucket

A nautical ditty bag (or other small canvas tote) is sized right for a blow-dryer and is made to be hung.

In a String Bag

You can also get creative and use just about any bag: we love the look of French market totes.

Freestanding Storage in the Bathroom

Think beyond traditional bathroom furnishings. You can gain extra storage—and a bit of sculptural interest—by inserting hardworking items with a small footprint.

1 Short on drawer and cabinet space? Roll in a cart, such as this Raskog model from Ikea. Canvas Dopp kits contain medicine cabinet staples, and larger bottles are neatly gathered in a tool caddy on the top tier.

2 Consider placing a wooden coatrack in a corner. In addition to holding bathrobes, it can be draped with baskets and bags (for towels, blow-dryers, and other accessories).

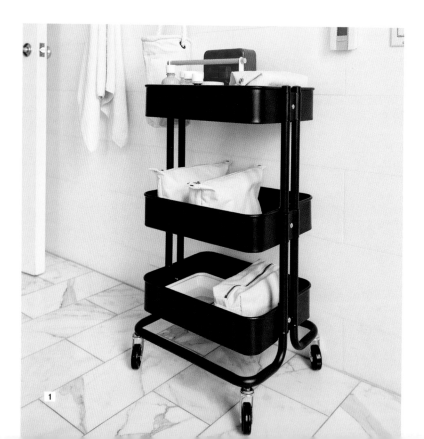

EXPERT ADVICE

Think Like a Hotelier

Hoteliers have to distill a household's worth of essentials into compact guest quarters—while keeping everything findable and presentable. We especially admire the way they treat necessities, such as tissue boxes and blow-dryers, in postage-stamp-size baths. Here are five tips from **Ray Pirkle,** hotel industry veteran and co-owner of the Rivertown Lodge in Hudson, New York.

1 **Install wall hooks in any available space.** In a bathroom, you want at least two hooks next to the shower for towels, one on the back of the door (a strong mount for a bathrobe), and another to the right beneath the sink (for hanging a hair dryer, makeup bag, or toiletry kit). Bonus points: prime and paint hooks the same color as the wall, so they all but disappear. (Be sure to paint the screw heads, too.)

2 **If you can see it or touch it, it should be an enjoyable experience.** So take time to make selections that not only work but are also good-looking and durable. Replace a cheap plastic toilet seat with a high-quality one; install a magnifying mirror; choose a well-made toilet brush and trash bin; add a metal light switch cover in place of a plastic one.

3 **Cover up what you don't want to look at.** Tuck your tissue box into an attractive container. Store toilet paper in a basket. Hang your hair dryer in a canvas bag on the back of the door or stow it in a flannel sack on a tray. Simple solutions can make a big visual difference.

4 **Consider adding wall-mounted shampoo and soap dispensers in the shower.** These streamline your products and make use of otherwise empty space.

5 **Create unity with your accessories.** Hotels are relaxing partly because they're free of clutter. On your sink top, you can achieve this tidy look by replacing a mix of containers with a matching set.

The Bathroom

The Cl

Closet

othes

At Remodelista, our interest in good design extends to our wardrobes. Regardless of our closet sizes, we swear by a pared-back collection of outfits that have become uniforms. Keeping only the true favorites allows us to see what we've got and makes getting pulled together fast and stress-free. If we haven't worn something in the last year, we store it or give it away. And we treat our belongings with old-fashioned valet-style care (see "Clothes Care Basics" on page 107). Of course, we, too, have our share of closet challenges. Here's how we tackle them.

STEAL THIS LOOK

A Well-Ordered Closet

Fitted with floor-to-ceiling storage, this closet holds a wardrobe's worth of clothing. Canvas bins, wire baskets, cardboard boxes, and metal dividers—most from the office and kitchen supplies departments of the Container Store and Ikea—make the shelf storage much more efficient. (See "The Remodelista Storage 75," beginning on page 162, for sourcing.) Here's why this setup works.

1 **Jumble-preventing bins and baskets** create discrete storage zones on open shelves.

2 **Piles of jeans, sweaters, and T-shirts limited to six per stack** prevent implosion. (We learned this from shop owner Eva Dayton; read more tips from her on page 121.)

3 **Organizational tools stolen from the office and kitchen** (a metal desktop sorter, left, and a pot lid rack, right) keep bags and clutches in tidy order.

4 **Metal-rimmed paper key tags** serve as labels on bins and baskets and allow for easy sorting.

5 **Neatly folded tops and bottoms** are organized by type and color.

6 **Glass-fronted drawers** are a bespoke detail worth copying: they protect shoes while enabling you to see what you've got.

7 **A Nicolle industrial kitchen** stool provides a place to put on shoes and drape clothes as you're getting dressed, and offers a way to reach high shelves.

The Secret to an Organized Closet

The most effective way to reorganize a closet, we've discovered, is to remove everything and put back only the best. So pile your closet contents on your bed and start sorting. Also, take the time to give the inside of your closet a thorough vacuuming. When going through clothes, a helpful question to ask yourself is: "Will I miss this?" The nos should be given away posthaste. Stow items you're not sure about in a box that you revisit in a month. Chances are, most will no longer have your name on them. As for items that don't fit or are in need of repair, put those in the question mark bin, too: if after three months the situation remains the same, out they go. Then restock the closet, following the six guidelines below.

1 **Use matching hangers.** You'll fit more in, and your closet will look much tidier.

2 **Opt for wooden hangers.** Wood is natural—something to always consider when choosing materials. It's also sturdy and looks good. Pair with cedar hanger discs to ward off moths.

3 **Group clothes according to type, color, and length.** This makes it easy to scan your wardrobe and zero in on what you're looking for.

4 **Keep only in-season clothes in your closet.** What you wear daily should take center stage. Store the other items in another closet, in canvas containers, or on a freestanding rack (see page 115).

5 **Space, don't cram, hangers.** So your clothes hang well and have room to breathe, leave regular gaps: a width of three fingers between items is a good general rule.

6 **Create a section for empty hangers.** When you take out an article of clothing, move the hanger to a designated parking area in your closet so you can always find a hanger when you need one.

The No-Closet Solution: 3-Tiered Bedroom Storage

Even in a tiny bedroom, chances are good there's extra space that can be colonized. Look up and look down (and in between), and insert drawers and pegs or hooks strategically. You'll gain the storage you need, and there's no crowding required.

High: Take a tip from the Shakers and line your walls with peg rails (see page 33 for more ingenious Shaker ideas). In the bedroom opposite, rails installed 5½ feet off the ground are used to hang not just clothes but all sorts of things, including jewelry and bags.

Mid-level: Wall-mounted to free up floor space, the bedside table opposite is a floating design from CB2. Its flip-down front conceals bedtime essentials.

Low: A bed can double as a dresser. The wooden storage bed below—from environmentally responsible furniture company Urban Green of Brooklyn— provides a remarkable amount of drawer space. The drawers hold pajamas and slippers under the head of the bed; bedding and towels on the side with the most floor space; and shoes on the other side. (See "Beds with Built-In Drawers" on page 201 for details and more options.)

Clothes Care Basics

We believe in buying clothes that are made to last, and taking good care of your wardrobe goes hand in hand with that philosophy. In addition to an iron, we recommend keeping a kit stocked with a small battery of butler-style tools, such as suit and lint brushes, for maintaining textiles (brushing and airing fabric is much gentler on clothes—and on the environment—than frequent dry cleanings), and sewing supplies for mending holes and replacing missing buttons. For warding off moths, deploy cedar in a number of guises.

The Essentials

- Lint brush

- Suit brush

- Sewing basics (pins and needles, thread, buttons, snaps, tape measure)

- Cedar blocks, hanger discs, and sachets

- Iron

- Ironing board (in a closet, consider a compact one installed on a wall or door)

Also Consider

- Spray bottle of lavender-scented ironing water

- Sweater stones (blocks of natural pumice that remove pills from knitwear)

- The Laundress Wash & Stain Bar for spot-cleaning

Where to Keep Your Shoes

To avoid a free-for-all on your closet floor, you need a system, and we've found that elevating shoes on shelves or stowing them in drawers works best—the shoes don't take up as much space as they would in boxes, and you don't have to hunt for the pair you're after. The shelves needn't be expensive: they're a staple at Ikea and the Container Store.

1 Hanging canvas shoe organizers make great use of vertical closet space. They're also much more orderly looking than door-hung shoe pockets.

2 To add maximum shoe storage to your closet, consider incorporating an Elfa kitchen cart from the Container Store into the mix; its graduated drawers work well for everything from flat sandals to boots.

3 Typically used for stowing clothes and blankets, under-the-bed drawers are also great for shoes. A space saver we learned from a fashion industry veteran with small closets: arrange pairs so that one is facing front and the other back for a yin-yang match; they fit more tightly this way.

1

2

3

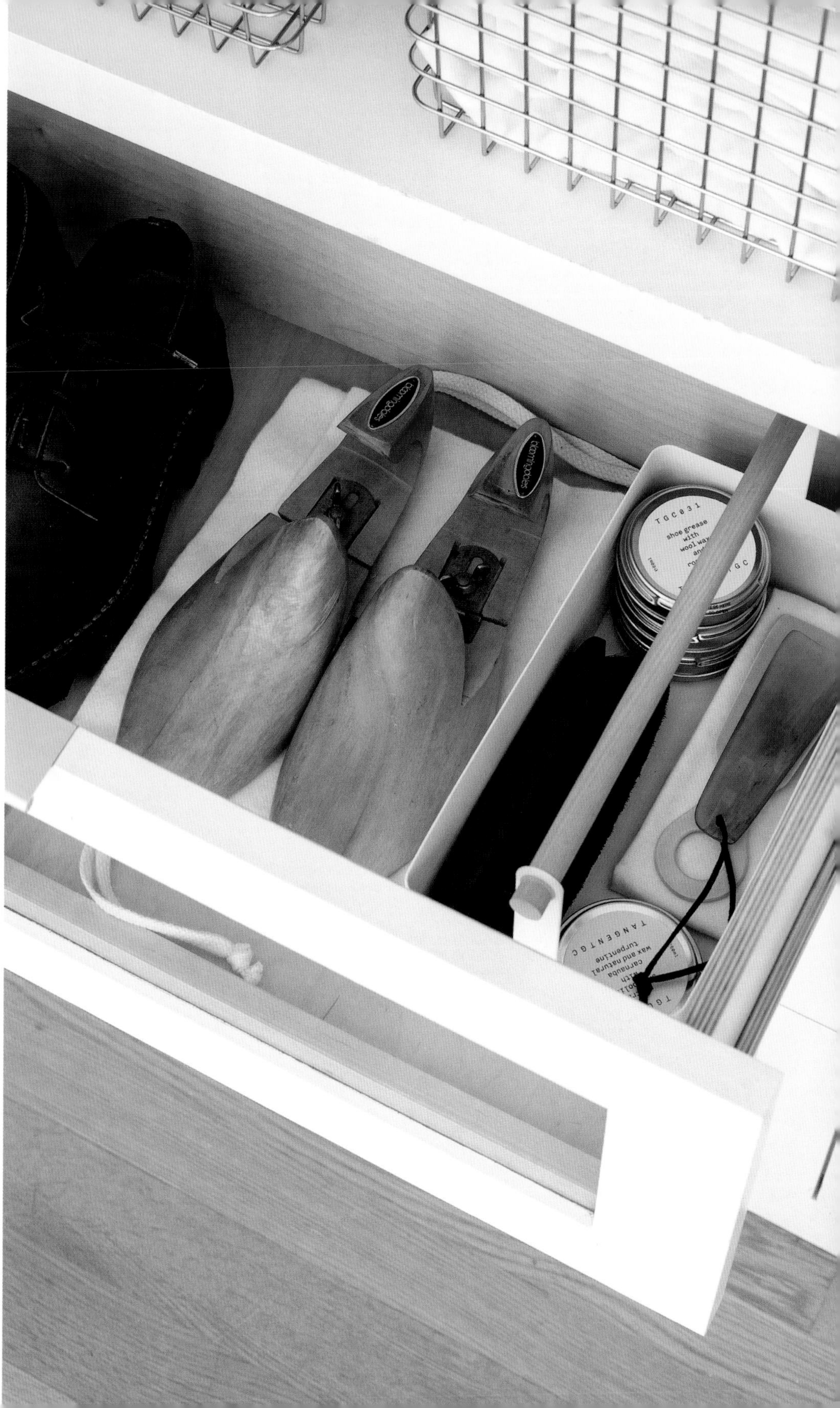
T G C 0 3 1
shoe grease
with
T A N G E N T G C

Shoe Care Basics

Cleaning and polishing shoes at home was standard practice until recently and deserves a comeback. Create a well-stocked kit—it can go in a drawer or box—and extend the life of your leather footwear. Shining shoes is quick and satisfying, and it makes a big impact. Leather gets dry and cracked if it's not cared for, but when maintained, it miraculously repels water while allowing air and moisture to escape (which is why it works so well on our feet). And, after all, you can tell a lot about a person by his or her shoes.

The Essentials

- Saddle soap (leather cleaner)

- Leather balm

- Shoe polish in neutral, black, and brown (we like the natural polishes from Tangent GC of Sweden)

- Shoe grease (for waterproofing)

- Shoe brush with soft natural bristles (for applying saddle soap)

- Shoe brush with stiff natural bristles (for cleaning off dust and for buffing)

- Cotton rag (for cleaning; a square from an old T-shirt is perfect)

- Buffing cloth

- Shoehorn

Also Consider

- Cedar shoe care box with built-in foot stand

- Wooden shoe trees (to absorb moisture and maintain the shape of your shoes)

Use Office and Kitchen Organizers in the Closet

Outfit your closet with clever organizers sourced from elsewhere; sometimes the best storage solutions come from unexpected sources.

Metal Desktop Sorter

For gathering handbags and clutches, think outside the closet: An upright office file rack is perfect for holding purses. (See "The Remodelista Storage 75," page 176, for sources.)

Pot Lid Holder

Standing metal pot lid organizers are easy to come by (this telescoping version is from Ikea; Amazon also has a range). The size and vertical partitions, we've discovered, make them just right for lining up purses and clutches.

File Rack

An accordion file holder keeps a supply of folded button-downs at the ready. The design is a take on the Flex-i-File, an office classic dating from 1941 that expands and contracts as needed. (See "The Remodelista Storage 75," page 176, for sources.)

Wooden Pegboard

Like trays, pegboards can be used to give loose pieces an organized place to belong. All you need is a patch of wall space, a board sized to fit (this one is by Block; see another option on page 125), and a hook or wall anchor.

The Clothes Closet

An Out-of-Season Clothes Rack

If you have a storage room but lack closet space, a freestanding rack can be used to hold your off-season wardrobe. (This design, made of ash and steel, is the Toj by Normann Copenhagen.)

To ensure that your clothes fare well, use cotton garment covers instead of plastic; they protect fabric from dust and light and allow air to circulate. The Butler's Closet makes chemical-free versions that are up to museum standards; more affordable canvas options are also easy to find. Gym-style wire baskets are great for rounding up everything from hats and gloves to boots. And a hanging sweater organizer can hold shoes in flannel bags, boots, accessories—in other words, more than just woolens.

The Frequent-Flyer Carry-On Pack

Eliminate last-minute packing panic by keeping a kit of small items at the ready. These can range from the essential—your passport (it should have a permanent home here, so you never have to hunt for it)—to extras that help smooth the way.

The Essentials

- Passport

- Travel toothbrush and toothpaste in a zippered pouch

- Travel wallet for foreign currency, tickets, and receipts

- Foreign currency (saved from past trips)

- Plug adapters for other countries

- Foldable shopping tote

Also Consider

- Homemade plane care package, including Aesop Ginger Flight Therapy— a cure for motion sickness/ general pick-me-up—eye mask, earplugs, and socks

- Melatonin (as a jet lag preventative, if you're a believer) in an art supply jar

- Travel umbrella

- Travel-size toiletries

- Mini sewing kit

- U.S. hundred-dollar bill (per our peripatetic photographer Matthew Williams, "A hundred bucks will get you out of just about any travel pinch, especially if you're traveling off the grid")

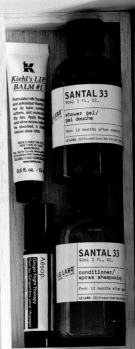

Nesting Suitcases

Suitcases are major space hogs—unless you take advantage of their hollow interiors. Consider investing in a nesting set; here, a Victorinox carry-on fits perfectly inside a larger bag from the same line. Most major suitcase companies offer nesting options for both hard and soft cases, some that hold as many as three bags in one. So if you have a lot of luggage, consider consolidating it. And use the empty inner case to store shoe bags, zippered packing cubes, and stocked toiletry kits. With these things and your travel kit (see the preceding pages) at the ready, you have one foot out the door.

Think Like a Boutique Owner

Clothes in stores are arrayed for maximum appeal. Your wardrobe can be, too. For advice on storing, stacking, and displaying, we turned to **Eva Dayton**, stylist, closet curator, and owner of Consignment Brooklyn. Here are her seven favorite tips.

1 **Take advantage of dead closet space.** Small closets often have unused ceiling and floor space that is perfect for installing hooks, shelves, or cubbies. And the shallow space on the back of closet doors is just right for belt and tie racks (you can make your own from hardware store wooden dowels).

2 **Use sturdy hangers.** Your garments will fare better: "Well-made hangers with rounded edges support the clothes they hold," says Dayton. She herself uses only white-painted wooden hangers.

3 **Display T-shirts so the labels face outward.** "This way you can keep track of what's what and find what you're after," Dayton says. She recommends folding the traditional way: turn the shoulders in and then the bottom up.

4 **Display sweaters with the labels away from you;** it's much easier to differentiate sweaters than T-shirts.

5 **Limit stacks of folded garments.** Beyond six or seven items, they start to spill over and get messy.

6 **Consider hanging a few whole outfits together.** Dayton says it "makes getting dressed super easy."

7 **Create a mini vanity in your closet.** Dedicate an open shelf to favorite things: jewelry, perfume, mementos. Set in a closet, it corrals items you reach for daily and provides a visual pick-me-up.

The
Work

station

A desk is a luxury in these laptop-as-office days.
If you're lucky enough to have one, turn it into your
hub of operations. And keep it spic-and-span: when
your desk is orderly, your mind is orderly. Think
you don't have room for a workspace? You actually
do—read on and we'll show you.

STEAL THIS LOOK

A Small but Clever Home Office

A simple Ikea desk and wall-mounted pegboard provide all the storage needed in this orderly office. Here's why it works.

1 **A pegboard by Kreisdesign** offers movable shelves.

2 **Flowers in a bud vase** from Heath Ceramics bring a touch of color and natural vitality into the space.

3 **Metal document boxes** hold essential files (see "The Remodelista Storage 75," page 167, for sourcing).

4 **The Alex desk from Ikea,** a perennial favorite, has built-in cable management (turn to page 133 to see how the cords are controlled).

5 **Eames meets Ikea.** A splurge-worthy classic, the Aluminum Group Management Chair is the ultimate in comfort.

6 **Ceramic vase as pencil holder.** Note that all of the accessories are made of sturdy—and nice to look at—natural materials.

7 **Flatware dividers** from the kitchen keep the desk drawers organized.

8 **A Uashmama paper basket** holds paper recycling (see "The Remodelista Storage 75," page 167, for sourcing.)

5

STEAL THIS LOOK

A Disappearing Desk

For tight quarters, consider a ship-style table that lifts up for use.
Here's why this one works.

1 **A shelf that becomes a table.** Ikea's drop-leaf Norberg design is
hinge-mounted on the wall. When the top is up, it's a desk; when it's
lowered, it becomes a shallow shelf.

2 **The surprisingly generous tabletop** is big enough for a laptop; it
also works as a dining table for two.

3 **Desk accessories** line up on the shelf, which remains in place
when the desk is folded down.

4 **A chair with a slim silhouette,** the industrial French Nicolle, pairs
well with the fold-down desk.

5 **An Original BTC Hector clip light** hangs from a Bed Bath &
Beyond metal towel ladder, another adaptable design that stands
ready to hold magazines and even sweaters and jackets.

5 Things to Get Rid of in the Home Office

1 Stray papers . . .

2 . . . followed by any now-empty file folders and cabinets.

3 Obsolete computer equipment, cords to nowhere, and other digital dinosaurs.

4 Excess pens and pencils, plus duplicate scissors and other tools.

5 Your datebook. We've embraced digital calendars and to-do lists. You should, too. For starters, they're always at your fingertips and help you get the work done (by sending you reminders, for instance).

For good ways to unload unwanted things, see pages 194–198.

Paper Is Passé: Whittle Down Your Holdings to a Few Hanging Files

Keep at least one file drawer or crate for legal papers (such as your mortgage documents or apartment lease, tax-related records, and your will). Label manila folders to hold these essentials. All else can be digitized and neatly arranged in your computer. Of course, paper still creeps in, but it needn't pile up on your desk. Pin school notices to a family bulletin board. And stow sentimental things, such as letters and old photos, in labeled boxes on a high closet shelf.

The No-Office Solution

Tactics for getting down to work at home and on the fly.

If the Sofa Is Your Workspace

Eliminate cord blight in your living room by turning your sofa into a charging station. Snake your chargers under your sofa cushions (you can go further and actually drill a hole in the frame if you're so inclined), and tuck a power strip underneath to hide the unsightlies.

If the Coffee Shop Is Your Workspace

Create a portable office in a tote. Fill it with zippered canvas pouches in various sizes to serve as mobile drawers, keeping your basics—laptop, notebooks, chargers, and pens and pencils—contained and easy to find.

How to Corral the Cords

You can't get rid of your cables, but you can coax them into presentability.

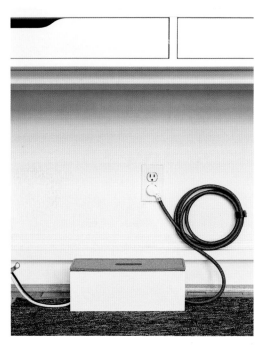

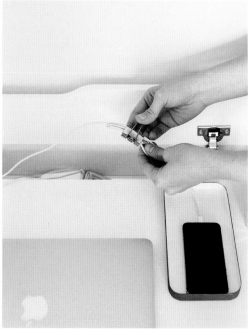

Deploy a Trap

Hide the cords snaking underfoot by capturing them in a box. This one is Ikea's Kvissle cable management box, but you can easily create your own by customizing a crate or shoebox with a cutout cord opening.

Tame the Unruly

Stop cords from taking over your desk. When chargers are too long, coil the excess and nip it with a metal clip or leather snap ring.

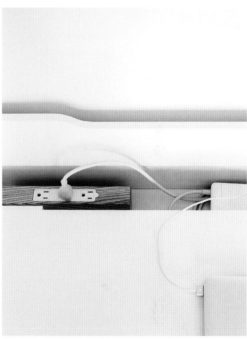

Offer Guidance

Affixed to the back of the desk, a metal clip can be used to direct a cord straight to the power source.

Opt for Built-Ins

Conveniently, Ikea's Alex desk (shown in full on page 125), is one of the many desks fitted with a cord hutch in the back. The wooden power strip is the Niko by Most Modest.

Minimize the TV

Keep the screen on view and all else hidden. Here are two over-the-mantel approaches, plus an instant pocket for the remotes.

A Built-In Niche

By taking advantage of a hollow wall over a mantel, designer Michaela Scherrer created an unobtrusive place for a TV. The cable box is hidden in a cardboard box under a tower of magazines.

Top-of-the-Closet Hideaway

A shelf or cabinet near a television provides an opportunity for all the cords and boxes to be consolidated. Pro tip: Amazon Prime offers a quick and affordable TV cord-mounting service. In this case, a specialist inserted a conduit behind the TV to hide the bundled wires, which are threaded into the closet where the cable box and other equipment lives.

Remote Control

Remotes tend to be visible when you don't want them to be—such as when you're entertaining—and buried when you need them. Remedy the situation by giving your remotes a handy place to live within reaching distance. For our sofa-side storage pocket, all you need is a ten-dollar cotton clothespin bag clipped to a sofa arm; fill with remotes and camouflage with a throw blanket.

The Workstation

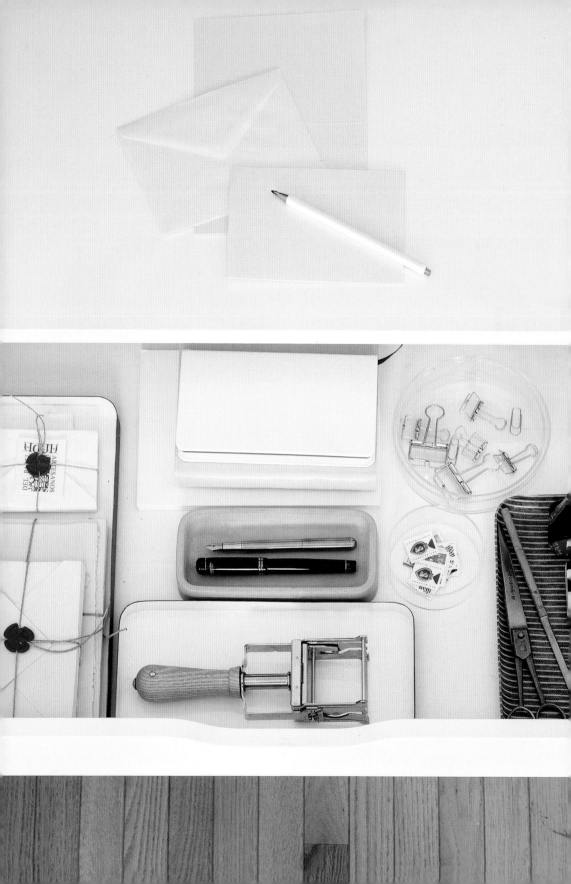

PREPAREDNESS KIT

The Good-Etiquette Drawer

Better behavior via stationery. When you have the supplies close at hand, you're far more likely to write that dinner party thank-you, birthday card, or note to a friend.

The Essentials

- Cards

- Envelopes

- Pens

- Postage stamps

- Trays and clear glass containers for corralling small items (see "The Remodelista Storage 75," pages 187 and 181, respectively)

Also Consider

- Return address stamp (this one is by Wms & Co.)

- Letter opener

- Fountain pen and ink

- Sealing wax and matches

- Scissors

- Brass paper clips and binder clips

Think Like a Stylist

Stand back and assess what you've got on display as if looking through a camera lens. Are too many objects competing for attention? Are your favorites getting lost in the visual cacophony? Every surface doesn't need to be clear, but there ought to be an intentionality to your displays. Discover five tricks of the styling trade—from **Ayesha Patel**, a veteran stylist and *Martha Stewart Living* alum.

1 **Add order through subtraction.** On location, stylists start by removing all the small pieces in a room. With a blank slate, they can then assess the setting and reintroduce objects one by one.

2 **Play with scale.** Pleasing still lifes keep the eyes moving from one object to another. To achieve this dynamism, set up an invisible connect-the-dots structure of triangles and circles linking your arrangements.

3 **When a room looks too bare, add some potted plants or cut flowers.** Nature is transforming: it instantly adds life.

4 **To minimize clutter, consider a monochromatic palette.** White, in particular, has a simplifying and cleansing effect. True, it takes discipline to live with only shades of pale, but your rooms will automatically look less busy, no matter how much is in them.

5 **Use trays as a finishing detail.** Trays imply graciousness and, as we've previously noted, supply that little bit of boundary that adds coherence. Patel keeps her home office on a large tray on the dining table: "It holds receipts (under a pretty rock) and small trays containing scissors, a letter opener, a stapler, and paper clips. It looks good, and when company is coming, I just pick it up and move it."

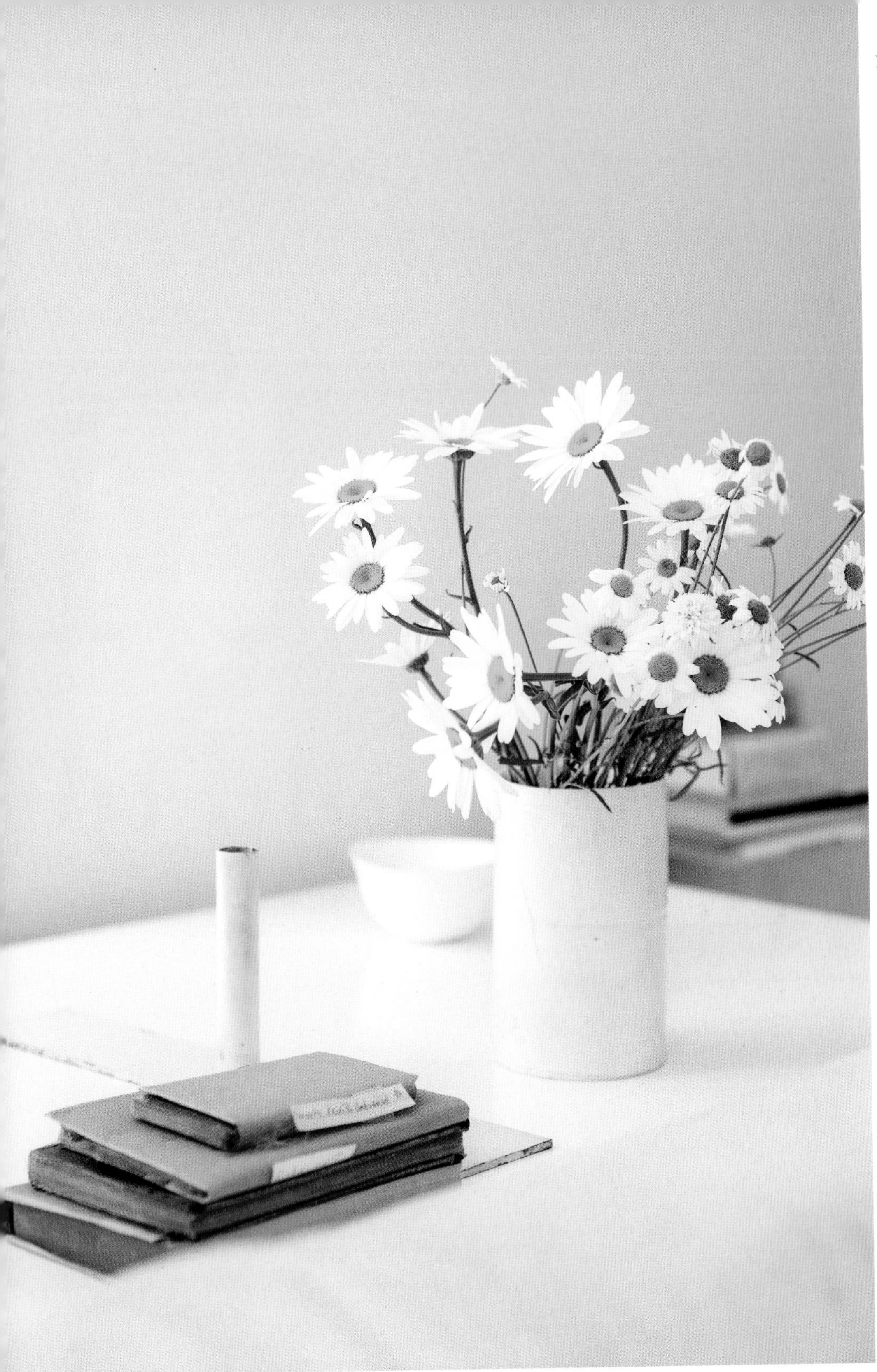

The L

and the

aundry
Utility Closet

A spotless, orderly laundry room is one of life's great luxuries. If you have your own washing machine and dryer, enhance the setup with simple, well-planned storage that makes cleaning clothes easy and satisfying. The same goes for your utility goods, whether they're part of your laundry or live elsewhere: give your broom, mop, and cleaning supplies a home that's useful and beautiful. All you need is a wall or a door. Hard to picture? Take a look.

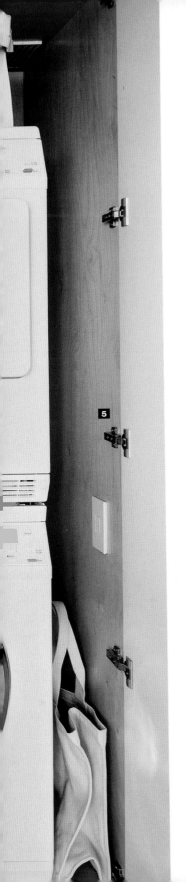

An Elegant All-in-One Laundry Closet

This compact laundry designed by architect Solveig Fernlund has birch plywood shelves and drawers for all the essentials. There's also room for general cleaning supplies, electronics, and a fold-up ironing board tucked into the side—all within an 8-by-5-foot space that can be hidden behind closed doors. Here's why it works.

1 **Decanted laundry detergent** is stored in a stainless steel *fusto* stolen from the kitchen (turn the page for details).

2 **A galvanized metal bucket** holds household cleaning supplies in a portable kit.

3 **Made-to-last natural materials:** from the wood-handled clothes brushes to the woolen dryer balls, just about everything is plastic-free and nice not only to look at but also to use.

4 **Laundry essentials** are sorted by function in a combination of shelves and drawers.

5 **Hinged doors** completely conceal the laundry.

6 **Bonus storage:** The hard-to-reach top shelf is put to good use as a home for Wi-Fi equipment.

An Old-World Soap Station

In this laundry setup, a *fusto* (a traditional Italian dispenser for olive oil, vinegar, and wine) functions as a liquid detergent dispenser. An S hook suspended on the spout provides a place to hang an enamelware measuring cup, and its leather cord is long enough to reach the washing machine.

Drying Racks, High and Low

Environmentalists and fabric-care experts agree: air-dry as much as you can. Not only is it the no-brainer green approach, but it also spares your clothes the ravages of being tumbled in the heat.

1 An Amish rack from Rejuvenation folds up when not in use.

2 To keep your floor space open, opt for the Sheila Maid Clothes Airer, shown in actress-turned-interior-designer Amanda Pays's Los Angeles laundry room. This ingenious contraption is lowered for loading clothes and raised to dry them in the warm air. (For sourcing, see page 203.)

The "Now You See It, Now You Don't" Laundry

You don't need a suburban-scaled laundry room: consider carving out a laundry in a hallway or kitchen.

1   In a modern-rustic kitchen designed by British cabinetmakers Plain English, the washing machine is elevated off the ground in a simple cabinet and concealed behind a wooden door. A wooden counter serves as a laundry folding surface.

2   Sliding mahogany panels (made by architect Lindon Schultz from salvaged 1940s office doors) camouflage a washing machine and dryer in artist-designer Christina Kim's downtown LA loft.

2

The Instant Utility Closet

A well-ordered cleaning closet (or wall) makes housekeeping chores easier to tackle, and it will also brighten your day. Create your own using a peg rail and a few trusty tools: select things that, to paraphrase Michael Pollan, your grandmother would recognize.

1 In the corner of a closet, a steel band of wall hooks by Room & Board forms a laundry wall. The wooden ironing board is from Williams-Sonoma. (See a clever second use for the canvas clothespin bag on page 135.)

2 Mounted on a closet door, an oak Shaker rail (from the Container Store) holds a lineup of basics. And in the closet, to maximize use of space, a vacuum is stowed atop an Elfa cart (also from the Container Store).

2

1

2

3

The Underworld: Chart New Territory Beneath Your Sink

If you're currently harboring your own circle of hell in your undercounter cabinets, take everything out, add a shelf liner for a clean slate, and consider introducing some of these storage tricks.

1 Make garbage bags easy to access and to look at: create a DIY roll dispenser by installing metal brackets and a dowel on an inside wall of your cabinet.

2 Avoid the familiar under-the-sink pileup by elevating some of your essentials. String an Ikea wire curtain rod (the same one shown on pages 44–45) to create a mini laundry line. Hang spray bottles and clip on cleaning towels. A generous metal bucket is a good container for additional cleaning tools.

3 Having a ready supply of cloth towels—and a place to stow the used ones—makes it much easier to do without paper towels. Here, a pair of Korbo wire baskets provides a place for clean and dirty cleaning cloths (and makes it easy to transport them to the washing machine).

PREPAREDNESS KIT

The Portable Cleaning Station

Cleaning is therapeutic—especially when you have a collection of tools that are a pleasure to use. Think minimalist: clear out the cobwebby bottles and assemble the keepers in and around a portable kit. This one is conveniently tucked right under the sink.

The Essentials

- Metal housekeeper's bucket (see "The Remodelista Storage 75," page 170, for sources)

- Natural bristle and wood-handled scrub brushes

- All-purpose cleaning solution and grit remover (see page 157 for recipes)

- Cleaning cloths

Also Consider

- Japanese coir scrub brush (hang to dry from an S hook)

- Rolls of recycled paper towels

- Canvas tote for gathering reusable shopping bags

Decant Your (All-Natural) Cleaning Potions

Find cleaning solution bottles at kitchen supply stores, or better yet, retrieve a couple from your own recycling bin. First, remove the labels—we use cooking oil to vanquish sticky residue. Then add bartender's pour spouts (also available from kitchen supply stores) or spray tops (these fit on most standard-size bottles and can be reused).

And while we're on the subject of cleaning solutions, all you really need are two DIY basics, so get rid of the thicket of plastic bottles clogging the cabinet under your sink and make your own. Our recipes are below.

All-Purpose Household Cleaner

1 Combine equal parts white vinegar and water in a spray bottle.

2 Add a few drops of eucalyptus or lemon essential oil (in addition to adding a nice scent, these are natural disinfectants).

Grease and Grit Remover

1 Mix ⅔ cup baking soda and ½ cup liquid castile soap in a bowl to dissolve lumps.

2 Dilute with ½ cup water and 2 tablespoons white vinegar.

3 Pour into a spray or pour bottle and shake before using.

Organize Your Pet Accessories

Animals are messy, but their gear doesn't have to be if you create designated spots for it.

1 Incorporate a place for your dog's daily necessities in your entry or mudroom, but keep even the lowliest details presentable. An old-fashioned cloth rag bag, for instance, is perfect for stowing pet waste bags, and it's a cut above the default plastic grocery bag. (You can buy a linen sack like ours—it's by Fog Linen—or stitch your own.)

2 An idea worth copying in the kitchen: an island designed by architect Oliver Freundlich cleverly incorporates a dog bowl niche. Out of sight, out of mind—and unlikely to get kicked over.

3 Give your cat an elegant place to dine. An enamelware flour bin holds cat food and a scoop next to a tray with glass bowls set on a small washable runner. Close the bag with metal office clips.

4 Decant dog food, too. Inexpensive, effective, and so much nicer looking than plastic, an old-fashioned metal trash bin is a perfect kibble container.

Think Like a Ship Designer

There's no wasted room in marine design—since quarters are tight, storage has to be tucked in here and there. It also has to be built to last (otherwise salt air and humidity take over). These five gracefully no-nonsense solutions, provided by **Asa Pingree**, a furniture designer and second-generation boatbuilder from North Haven, Maine, can be applied to compact quarters of all sorts, on land and at sea.

1 **Use every square inch.** Look for cavities in your home and ask yourself: "How can I gain access to that and put it to work?" Pingree says. The risers under stairs? Insert drawers. The space under a bench? Add a hinged seat and you have a bin. The hollow under the floorboards? Create a trapdoor.

2 **Choose furnishings that fold, stack, or disappear.** On a ship, tables drop down from the wall on hinges, so they're out of the way when not in use. Teak and canvas chairs fold up. So do canvas buckets.

3 **Install hardware that's flush with the walls.** Knobs that stick out are a hazard in tight quarters: as you move around, you're liable to get bumped. Discover the nautical alternative: flush-mounted ring pulls that are just as easy to install as standard cabinet hardware. No more bruises, and your rooms will feel streamlined.

4 **Embrace nautical hooks.** Unlike landlubber counterparts of plated metal, marine hooks are solid brass, steel, or bronze. Dock cleats work well for securing Roman shade cords and as hooks for hanging towels and robes. And they look good.

5 **Use canvas storage.** Canvas boat totes and buckets are handy all over the house. We hang them in the bathroom to hold toiletries, washcloths, and kids' bath toys. Source from nautical suppliers such as Hamilton Marine, and from All Hands, makers of the ditty bag shown opposite.

The
Remo
Stor

delista
age 75

Elevate the everyday by selecting thoughtfully designed, trend-proof household basics. Here's what you need to achieve a well-organized (and nearly plastic-free) existence.

Bags and Totes

01

Natural Cotton Canvas Zippered Pouches

USEFUL FOR: Keeping small items, such as medicine and other toiletries, in one tidy place.

AVAILABLE FROM: Beckel Canvas Products (beckelcanvas.com), Delfonics (sweetbellausa.com), Amazon (amazon .com), and various sellers on Etsy (etsy.com)

02

Cotton Canvas Clothespin Bag

USEFUL FOR: Introducing a pouch where you need one, whether hanging on a laundry line or draped over a sofa arm (for holding TV remotes).

AVAILABLE FROM: Augbunny and other sellers on Amazon (amazon.com)

03

Canvas Ditty Bag

USEFUL FOR: Keeping sailors' possessions near their bunks—and also for storing bath toys, washcloths, and other bathroom accessories.

AVAILABLE FROM: All Hands (allhandsny.com) and Hamilton Marine Supply (hamiltonmarine.com)

04
Canvas Boat Tote

USEFUL FOR: Carrying gear aboard your boat. Also great for keeping all your desktop accessories, laptop and charger included, in one portable bag.

AVAILABLE FROM: Steele Canvas (steelecanvas.com)

05
French Net Market Bags

USEFUL FOR: Toting produce and groceries as well as for hanging household items, such as hair dryers.

AVAILABLE FROM: Brook Farm General Store (brookfarmgeneralstore.com) and Ecobags (ecobags.com), among other sources

Baskets, Bins, and Containers

06
Verso Birch Baskets

USEFUL FOR: Household storage of all sorts. Verso baskets come in a range of sizes, making them ideal for filling with everything from apples to blankets. They have leather or felt handles, which are not only prettier than the standard handles but also more durable.

AVAILABLE FROM: Verso Design (www.versodesign.fi/en). For similar, American-produced designs made of ash, go to the Peterboro Basket Co. (peterborobasket.com).

07
Adirondack Baskets

USEFUL FOR: Shouldering picnic lunches and hiking gear as well as for hanging in a hall as a place to gather the day's mail or your baseball cap collection.

AVAILABLE FROM: The Birch Store (thebirchstore.com)

08
The Korbo Classic 80

USEFUL FOR: A clothes hamper (which can be purchased with a fitted cotton laundry bag in black or white).

AVAILABLE FROM: Finnish Design Shop (finnishdesignshop.com), Design Within Reach (dwr.com), and Scandinavian Design Center (scandinaviandesigncenter.com), among other sources

09
Wire Gym Baskets

USEFUL FOR: Holding your T-shirts, extra rolls of TP, onions and potatoes, and more.

AVAILABLE FROM: The Container Store (containerstore.com; left), and Schoolhouse Electric & Supply Co. (schoolhouseelectric .com; right)

10
Uashmama Paper Baskets

USEFUL FOR: Lightweight storage bins, wastebaskets, and luggable covers for potted plants made of a durable Tyvek-like material.

AVAILABLE FROM: Uashmama (shopuashmamausa.com)

11
Shaker Nesting Boxes

USEFUL FOR: Storing sewing things, kitchen ingredients, and any small parts.

AVAILABLE FROM: Makié (makieclothier .com), which sells Masashi Ifuji's finely crafted made-in-Japan version, shown here. Also available from Shaker Workshops (shakerworkshops.com), among other sources.

12
Italian Powder-Coated Steel Document Boxes

USEFUL FOR: Stylishly concealing paperwork and other desktop supplies.

AVAILABLE FROM: Sweet Bella (sweetbellausa.com)

13

Wooden Tissue Box Cover

USEFUL FOR: Camouflaging unattractive tissue boxes.

AVAILABLE FROM: Various Etsy sellers, including ColoriCrafts (etsy.com/shop/ColoriCrafts), as well as arts and crafts stores, such as Michaels (michaels.com), where it's sold for crafts projects. Nalata Nalata (nalatanalata.com) offers a refined Japanese version.

14

Bigso Box of Sweden Office Storage Boxes

USEFUL FOR: Handsome and sturdy storage for the desk and beyond. Made of recycled fiberboard.

AVAILABLE FROM: The Container Store (containerstore.com)

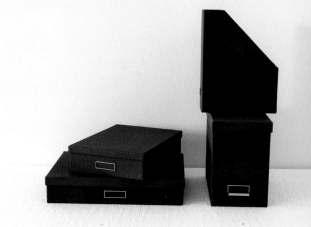

15

Wooden In-Out Box

USEFUL FOR: Keeping bills to pay in one place. Also works as a tray for tabletop things, such as place mats, cloth napkins, and cutlery.

AVAILABLE FROM: Office Supply (officesupply.com) and vintage sellers on Etsy (etsy.com) and elsewhere

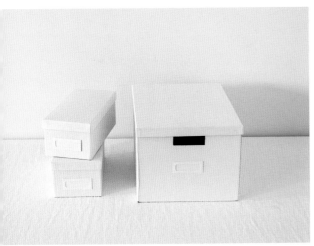

16
Ikea Tjena Series Boxes

USEFUL FOR: Labeling and storing letters, photos, files, fabric swatches, children's artwork, and countless other odds and ends.

AVAILABLE FROM: Ikea (ikea.com)

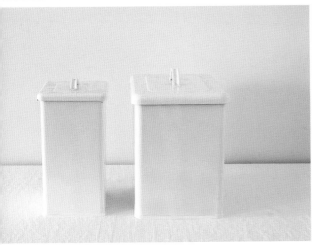

17
Enamelware Kitchen Bins

USEFUL FOR: Storing bread and countless other basics (see page 158).

AVAILABLE FROM: Garden Trading (gardentrading.co.uk) and vintage dealers on Etsy (etsy.com)

18
Yamazaki Tosca Toolbox

USEFUL FOR: Corralling everything from tools to toiletries to spices to craft supplies. It's made of steel with a wooden handle and comes in two sizes.

AVAILABLE FROM: Amazon (amazon.com), Wayfair (wayfair.com), and Unison (unisonhome.com)

19
Housekeeper's Galvanized Bucket

USEFUL FOR: Downton Abbey–esque portable storage. Fill with under-the-sink essentials in the kitchen or bathroom, cleaning supplies, and gardening gear.

AVAILABLE FROM: Labour and Wait (labourandwait.co.uk). Enameled versions with swing handles are sold by Cost Plus World Market (worldmarket.com) and Garden Trading (gardentrading.co.uk).

20
Serax White Canvas Nesting Bins by Marie Michielssen

USEFUL FOR: Shelf organization all over, including closets, playrooms, and laundries.

AVAILABLE FROM: Serax (serax.com)

21
Canvas Bins with Labels

USEFUL FOR: Holding hats, gloves, and other accessories and small items on shelves in front halls, closets, and playrooms.

AVAILABLE FROM: The Container Store (containerstore.com)

22
Steele Canvas Truck

USEFUL FOR: Corralling laundry as well as toys, blankets and pillows, and garage gear. Made by a family-owned Boston company, Steele Canvas carts come in a range of sizes and are strong enough to carry bricks around construction sites.

AVAILABLE FROM: Steele Canvas (steelecanvas.com)

Clips and Closures

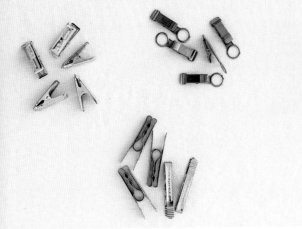

23
Small Metal Clips

USEFUL FOR: Creating storage opportunities all over, including for hanging kitchen towels, taming electrical cords, affixing prints to the wall, and consolidating papers.

AVAILABLE FROM: Present and Correct (presentandcorrect.com), Labour and Wait (labourandwait.co.uk), and Museum of Useful Things (museumofusefulthings.com)

24
Ellepi Colored Metal Clips

USEFUL FOR: Bundling papers as well as securing electrical cords while introducing a hint of glossy color.

AVAILABLE FROM: Sweet Bella (sweetbellausa.com)

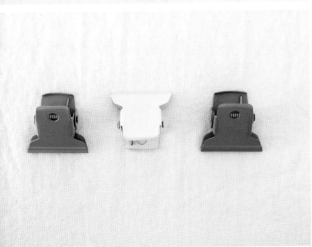

25

Mawa by Reston Lloyd
Rubber-Tipped Metal Clip
Hangers

USEFUL FOR: Hanging handbags, wet bathing suits, and myriad other things.

AVAILABLE FROM: Reston Lloyd (restonlloyd.com) and Amazon (amazon.com)

26

Wooden Clothespins

USEFUL FOR: Attaching cards to presents, holding plant stems in place, marking whose cloth napkin and towel is whose (by labeling or color-coding the clothespin itself), and, of course, hanging laundry.

AVAILABLE FROM: The Home Depot (homedepot.com) and Staples (staples.com), among other sources. The Container Store (containerstore.com) sells mini versions.

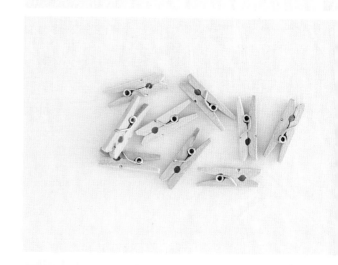

27

Natural Rubber Ties and
Rubber Bands

USEFUL FOR: Gathering bundles—of electrical cords, books, and other things. (The tie bands have a tab that holds them in place.)

AVAILABLE FROM: Labour and Wait (labourandwait.co.uk)

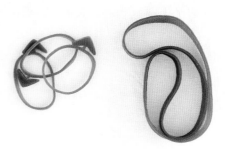

Closet Accessories

28
Wooden Hangers

USEFUL FOR: Orderly closets and well-maintained clothes. Consider color-coding: white hangers for tops, natural wood for pants.

AVAILABLE FROM: Bed Bath & Beyond (bedbathandbeyond.com), the Container Store (containerstore.com), and Ikea (ikea.com), among other sources

29
Umbra Hitch Accessory Organizer

USEFUL FOR: Looping over a closet rod or a hook as a hanger for handbags, totes, and belts.

AVAILABLE FROM: The Container Store (containerstore.com) and Umbra (umbra.com)

30
Zippered Canvas Storage Bag

USEFUL FOR: Storing off-season sweaters and other garments as well as blankets.

AVAILABLE FROM: Muji (in stores only), the Laundress (thelaundress.com), Fleabags' Immodest Cotton line (fleabg.com), and Cuddledown (cuddledown.com)

31

Butler's Closet Cotton Flannel Shoe Bags

USEFUL FOR: Protecting shoes from dust, dirt, and other shoes in closets and suitcases.

AVAILABLE FROM: The Butler's Closet (thebutlerscloset.com)

Drawer and Shelf Organizers

32

Bisley Five-Drawer Cabinet

USEFUL FOR: Corralling office accessories as well as many multipiece household items, including flatware. Bisley has been making steel storage in the UK since 1940.

AVAILABLE FROM: The Container Store (containerstore.com) in thirteen colors

33

Metal Flatware Tray

USEFUL FOR: Organizing cutlery so there's never any guesswork.

AVAILABLE FROM: Restaurant supply stores such as Web Restaurant Store (webrestaurantstore.com)

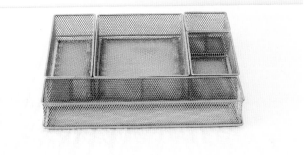

34

Design Ideas Mesh Drawer Organizers

USEFUL FOR: Injecting order and avoiding unused space. An instant remedy for the unruly junk drawer.

AVAILABLE FROM: Design Ideas (designideas.net), Amazon (amazon.com), and the Container Store (containerstore.com)

35

Natural Cotton Canvas Drawer Liner

USEFUL FOR: Creating a clean slate in drawer and cabinet bottoms. This liner is adhesive-free, but it has a nonslip backing. It comes in a roll; trim to fit.

AVAILABLE FROM: The Container Store (containerstore.com)

36

Ikea Variera Pot Lid Organizer

USEFUL FOR: Keeping pot lids orderly and in one place. The telescoping design also works for small bags, purses, and other flat items, and it adjusts to fit a range of drawer and shelf sizes.

AVAILABLE FROM: Ikea (ikea.com)

37

Cabinet Shelf Risers

USEFUL FOR: Maximizing space in kitchen cabinets, under sinks, and beyond by creating additional shelves.

AVAILABLE FROM: Hardware stores and the Container Store (containerstore.com)

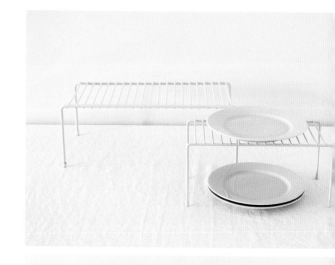

38

Silver Mesh Super Sorter

USEFUL FOR: Keeping letters, files, and notebooks in order. Shaped like an outsized toast rack, the sorter also neatly holds other flat, rectangular objects, such as handbags and purses.

AVAILABLE FROM: The Container Store (containerstore.com)

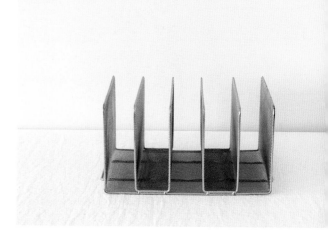

39

Zydeco File Sorter

USEFUL FOR: Storing files, mail, and magazines—and also folded button-down shirts. The Zydeco telescopes open and closes compactly.

AVAILABLE FROM: Design Ideas (designideas.net)

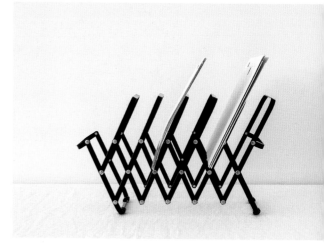

Hooks and Pegs

40

Hand-Forged Outsized Iron Nails and Metal Pushpins

USEFUL FOR: Hanging clothes, bags, dish towels—anything you want to keep off the floor—as well as for pinning papers to bulletin boards and securing artwork.

AVAILABLE FROM: Brook Farm General Store (brookfarmgeneralstore.com) and House of Antique Hardware (houseofantiquehardware.com)

41

Single Wooden Pegs

USEFUL FOR: Instant storage wherever you need it, such as in an entryway, inside a closet, or on a bedroom wall. We imported these from Germany; why aren't they available everywhere?

AVAILABLE FROM: Manufactum (manufactum.com)

42

S Hooks

USEFUL FOR: Looping on any rail or rod to create a hook. We use S hooks all over the house for hanging everything from dish towels to handbags.

AVAILABLE FROM: Hardware and building supply stores in a range of sizes, metals, and finishes. The heavy brass example shown here (on far left) is from New York design company Sir/Madam (sirmadam .com).

43

Scout Regalia Powder-Coated Steel SR Wall Hooks

USEFUL FOR: Hanging jackets, baseball caps, and key rings while adding a bit of color. These industrial-chic hooks have a low profile and a strong presence.

AVAILABLE FROM: Scout Regalia (scoutregalia.com) in six colors

44

The Dots from Muuto

USEFUL FOR: Introducing playful coat hooks and cabinet pulls that can be arranged in the pattern of your choosing. The Dots come in three sizes and twelve colors in addition to oiled oak (shown) and ash. And they feel great to the touch.

AVAILABLE FROM: Muuto (muuto.com) and many retailers. Create a similar look with unfinished cabinet pulls from the Home Depot (homedepot.com).

45

Stropp Hanging Peg

USEFUL FOR: Holding scarves, hand towels, and rolled-up newspapers and magazines.

AVAILABLE FROM: By Lassen (bylassen .com). Variations of this design are made by Mathilda Clahr (mathildaclahr.com) and Alice Tacheny (alicetacheny.com), among others.

Kitchen Containers

46

Glass Jars with Metal Screw Caps

USEFUL FOR: Storing herbs and spices in containers that line up like soldiers.

AVAILABLE FROM: The small (2-ounce) jars are from art stores, such as Blick (dickblick.com), where they're sold for mixing and storing paint. The taller (3-ounce) jars are from the Container Store (containerstore.com).

47

Weck Mold Jars

USEFUL FOR: Stackable, airtight storage. Designed in 1900 for preserving foods, Weck jars come in a range of sizes, all with wide mouths that are perfect for leftovers and decanted dry goods.

AVAILABLE FROM: Weck (weckjars.com), Williams-Sonoma (williams-sonoma.com), and Schoolhouse Electric & Supply Co. (schoolhouseelectric.com), to name but a few retailers

48

Canning Jars

USEFUL FOR: Storing leftovers as well as batches of tomato sauce and jam.

AVAILABLE FROM: Countless sources, including grocery and hardware stores. These are Korken jars from Ikea (ikea.com). For a full pantry organized around canning jars, see Blisshaus (blisshaus.com).

49

Glass Refrigerator Containers

USEFUL FOR: Storing leftovers. Popular since the days of the icebox, these versatile covered containers can also go from oven to table.

AVAILABLE FROM: Anchor Hocking (shown in back; oneida.com) and Pyrex (pyrex.com), but only with plastic tops of late. We like the vintage all-glass versions (shown in front) that are plentiful—and affordable—on Etsy (etsy.com) and eBay (ebay.com). Search for "glass refrigerator jars."

50

Biscuit Jars

USEFUL FOR: Storing flour, sugar, and other decanted pantry goods, including biscuits. Caveat: they're heavier than plastic—but also nicer looking; good on a counter rather than a high shelf.

AVAILABLE FROM: Anchor Hocking (oneida.com)

51

Tiffins

USEFUL FOR: Carrying multicourse lunches to school and work. Also ideal for storing leftovers.

AVAILABLE FROM: Indian food markets, Amazon (amazon.com), and Food 52 (food52.com/shop)

52

Muji White Porcelain Storage Containers

USEFUL FOR: Affordable, plastic-free, stackable food storage that's microwave and dishwasher safe. To keep track of contents, add washi tape labels.

AVAILABLE FROM: Muji (muji.com/us), in three sizes

53

Baum Storage Canisters by Kinto

USEFUL FOR: Creating stackable, streamlined storage. The glass is heat resistant and the wooden lid is fitted with a silicone ring for an airtight seal.

AVAILABLE FROM: Rakuten Global Market (global.rakuten.com/en) and Amazon (amazon.com)

54

Lab-Style Cylindrical Glass-Covered Containers

USEFUL FOR: Storing cotton balls, favorite earrings, and many other items.

AVAILABLE FROM: Makié (makieclothier .com), pictured. Other sources include Muji (muji.com/us), Schoolhouse Electric & Supply Co. (schoolhouse.com), Dover Street Market (doverstreetmarket.com), and labware vendors (see page 217).

55

Reusable Organic Cotton Mesh Produce Bags

USEFUL FOR: Breathable, plastic-free produce storage. Also handy for bringing to the market instead of using plastic bags.

AVAILABLE FROM: Simple Ecology (simpleecology.com) and many vendors on Etsy (etsy.com) and Amazon (amazon.com)

56

Linen Bowl Covers

USEFUL FOR: Keeping salads, soups, leftovers, and other bowls of food fresh—and free of flies. Made of double layers of washable linen edged with elastic trim, the covers are a tight-fitting (but not airtight) alternative to disposable wraps.

AVAILABLE FROM: Ambatalia (ambatalia .com) and Quitokeeto (quitokeeto.com)

57

Furoshiki Cloth

USEFUL FOR: Wrapping almost anything. Furoshiki is the centuries-old Japanese art of bundling: knot the ends to form a satchel for carrying produce from the market, and to serve as countertop storage. Also good as a gift-wrap alternative.

AVAILABLE FROM: Ambatalia (ambatalia.com)

58
Glass Dispensers

USEFUL FOR: Filling with hand soap, dish soap, homemade cleaning solutions (see page 157), and water.

AVAILABLE FROM: Amazon (amazon.com), Bed Bath & Beyond (bedbathandbeyond .com), and Etsy (etsy.com). Metal pour spouts and other inserts are also available for standard glass bottles (new or recycled).

Rails, Racks, and Pegboards

59
Ikea Ekby Wooden Shelf and Metal Brackets

USEFUL FOR: Introducing a shelf wherever you need one. The metal brackets come in black as well as white; prices start at two dollars.

AVAILABLE FROM: Ikea (ikea.com)

60
Block Pegboard

USEFUL FOR: Creating workbench-style storage all over the house (see an idea for the closet on page 113).

AVAILABLE FROM: Block (blockdesign.co.uk)

61
Shaker Peg Rail

USEFUL FOR: Introducing simple storage in every room. The Shakers showed that anything with a loop can (and should) be hung.

AVAILABLE FROM: The style shown here is from the Container Store (containerstore .com). Many other sources offer ready-made and custom peg rails, including Peg and Rail (pegandrailusa.com) and NH Woodworking (nhwoodworking.com).

62
Room & Board Spike Multiple Wall Hook

USEFUL FOR: Instant hanging power and presence. This powder-coated steel contemporary cousin to the Shaker rail comes in fourteen colors.

AVAILABLE FROM: Room & Board (roomandboard.com)

63
Ikea Grundtal Stainless Steel Rails

USEFUL FOR: Suspending over the kitchen counter as a hanging rack for pots, pans, tools, and accessories. The Grundtal is one of Ikea's cult items that has been artfully used in a range of culinary settings.

AVAILABLE FROM: Ikea (ikea.com)

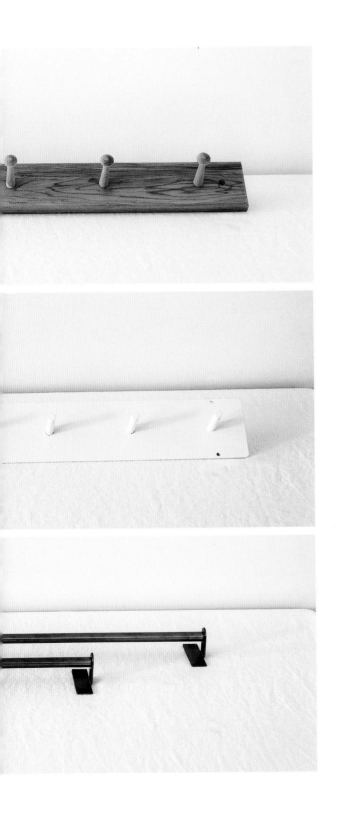

64

Riess Enamel Hanging Bars

USEFUL FOR: Storing metal ladles, skimmers, and other kitchen tools (which Riess of Austria also makes in white enamel). Riess rails can be put to other inventive uses, including as low-profile bathroom hand towel racks (see page 88).

AVAILABLE FROM: Labour and Wait (labourandwait.co.uk) and Objects of Use (objectsofuse.com)

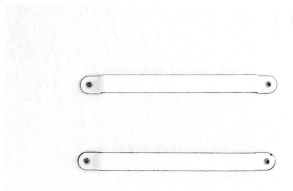

65

Umbra Adjustable Metal Drapery Brackets and Unfinished Wooden Dowel

USEFUL FOR: Hanging inside a cabinet as a dispenser for rolls of garbage bags or paper towels.

AVAILABLE FROM: Amazon (amazon.com) and Umbra (umbra.com)

Trays

66

Corin Mellor Willow Plywood Trays

USEFUL FOR: Serving food, assembling tableware, and creating a countertop bar. Corin Mellor's rimmed design is intended as a "sophisticated version of the familiar canteen tray."

AVAILABLE FROM: David Mellor (davidmellordesign.com)

67
Fog Linen Trays

USEFUL FOR: Introducing a base of orderly pattern to a group of objects. Made of linen and polyester resin, these trays are light and water resistant, and come in three sizes.

AVAILABLE FROM: Fog Linen (shop-foglinen.com)

68
Japanese Enamelware Trays

USEFUL FOR: Providing a clean, unobtrusive home for loose items anywhere in the house, both in drawers and cabinets and on view. These trays are at the top of our all-time favorite storage staples list.

AVAILABLE FROM: The Good Design Store at Dover Street Market (in stores only)

69
Artist's Palette Enamelware Trays

USEFUL FOR: Blending paint colors—and, like the more refined Japanese trays in the preceding entry, as anchors for everything from silverware to potted plants. Modeled after trays used by butchers, palette trays are easy to clean and durable (but be warned that they're prone to rim chips).

AVAILABLE FROM: Blick (dickblick.com). You can also find vintage examples by searching for "enamelware medical trays."

Utility Storage

70

Manila and Wooden Tags

USEFUL FOR: Hanging a label on all sorts of things, such as baskets and bins, key racks, and donations of household goods.

AVAILABLE FROM: Staples (staples.com) in classic manila and white, and sold as gift tags at the Container Store (containerstore.com)

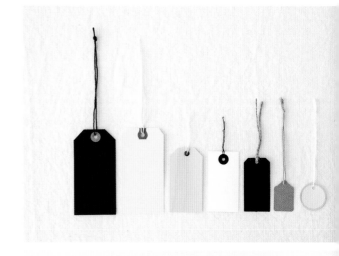

71

Rubber Bucket Made from Recycled Tires

USEFUL FOR: Storing rolled-up bath towels and other small objects in an arresting, repurposed design.

AVAILABLE FROM: Matsunoya (matsunoya.jp). Find a similar design at Baileys (baileyshome.com) and Viva Terra (vivaterra.com).

72

Stainless Steel Dock Cleats

USEFUL FOR: Hanging on walls and doors as hooks for towels, bathrobes, and marine canvas buckets filled with bath or utility products. Also good for securing Roman shade cords and other household pulleys (see page 161).

AVAILABLE FROM: West Marine (westmarine.com) and Amazon (amazon .com), among other sources

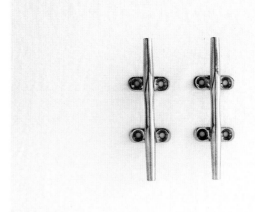

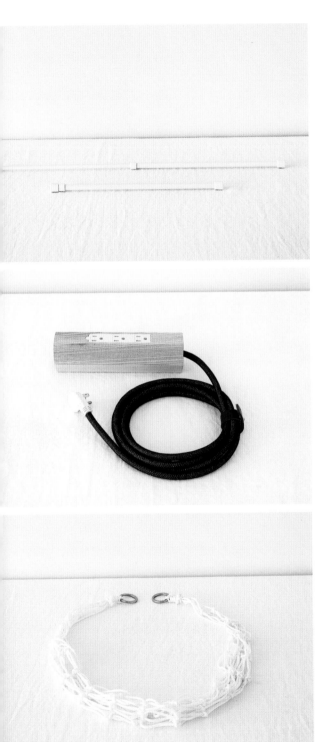

73
Tension Rods

USEFUL FOR: Hanging curtains, creating dividers within drawers, devising instant shoe shelves, and more: spring-loaded and expandable, tension rods can be put to countless DIY uses.

AVAILABLE FROM: Amazon (amazon.com), the Home Depot (homedepot.com), and hardware and building supply stores

74
Niko Power Strip by Most Modest

USEFUL FOR: Replacing unsightly multiplug outlets. Extending from a hexagonal wooden base, the 10-foot cord is cloth-covered and kept orderly with a leather clip.

AVAILABLE FROM: Most Modest (mostmodest.com)

75
Nautical Rope Storage Hammock

USEFUL FOR: Hanging in the bathroom and filling with bath toys. Storage hammocks have traditionally been used in sailors' bunks for keeping essentials within easy reach (and allowing them to air-dry).

AVAILABLE FROM: Best Made Co. (bestmadeco.com) and marine suppliers such as Defender (defender.com) and West Marine (westmarine.com)

Resou

rces

Too often, storage supplies are picked up on the fly
at big-box stores without thought to material or
design. But it doesn't have to be that way. In fact,
purchasing these things can be as satisfying as buying
new furniture and accessories—and much more
affordable—if you know where to get them. In this
section, we explain how to edit out household plastics;
provide a detailed directory of businesses and charities
to turn to when you're getting rid of unwanted goods;
and share our favorite sources for storage staples.

Alternatives to Plastic: Better Accessories for All Over the House

Plastic may be ubiquitous and affordable, but it's also an environmental scourge and, according to legions of studies, detrimental to your health. Here are some good alternatives.

INSTEAD OF	OPT FOR	NOTES
A plastic dish scrubber	A wood-handled brush with natural bristles	Traditional and compostable. Iris Hantverk and Bürstenhaus Redecker are two favorite brands available at Sur La Table and on Amazon.
A plastic drying rack	A stainless steel or wooden rack	Plastic components drag down a dish drainer. Go for a metal or bamboo countertop rack or, better yet, a wall-hung metal catchall (see page 60).
Synthetic sponges	Natural cellulose sponges	These are now for sale at supermarkets; we especially like the ones with loofah "scrubbies" on one side. To sanitize, put through the dishwasher or in the microwave (wet, for one minute).
Plastic bottles of dish soap and household cleaners	Glass dispensers	Dish soap can be decanted into just about anything lightweight and pourable—a glass soda bottle with a bar spout, for instance. (Of course, unless you make your own, you'll still have to buy the soap in a plastic bottle. See page 157 for our all-natural recipes.)
Tupperware-style food storage containers	Glass refrigerator containers, Mason jars, and stainless steel tiffins	Glass boxes are our favorite because they're stackable and you can see their contents (go to "The Remodelista Storage 75," page 180, for details). Mason and other canning jars come in a huge range of sizes. For carrying lunch, we recommend Indian stainless steel tiffins (see page 180).
Plastic wrap	Beeswax-infused cotton wrap, cloth bowl covers, and waxed paper	There are several nondisposable brands of wrap; Bee's Wrap is one. When airtightness isn't essential, Ambatalia cloth bowl covers (see page 182) are our pick. We also use plates as bowl and plate toppers.
Plastic food storage bags	Cloth produce bags and glass or metal containers	Etsy, Rodale's, and Amazon are three good sources.

INSTEAD OF	OPT FOR	NOTES
Acrylic polypropylene cutting boards	Wooden cutting boards	Scrub the wood clean with a paste of baking soda, salt, and water.
Plastic stirring spoons	Classic wooden chef spoons	These are available all over. Thanks to the current artisan renaissance, lovely hand-carved versions are also easy to find.
Plastic ladles, spatulas, and other basic cooking tools	Metal and wooden utensils	Newly popular in recent years, they're easy to find in cookware shops (or raid your parents' and grandparents' drawers).
Plastic water bottles	Stainless steel, titanium, or glass bottles	S'well and Klean Kanteen are but two good brands.
Plastic trays	Wooden or metal trays	See "The Remodelista Storage 75" (pages 186–187) for sources.
A plastic bucket	An enamelware or galvanized tin bucket	See "The Remodelista Storage 75" (page 170) for sources.
Plastic clothes hangers	Wooden hangers	Ikea and the Container Store both offer multiple affordable choices.
Plastic clothes storage bins	Zippered canvas bags	Find these at Muji and the Laundress, among other sources.
Plastic garment covers and dry cleaner's bags	Cotton or canvas covers	For chemical-free versions, go to an online source, such as the Butler's Closet.
Plastic laundry baskets	Wicker, rattan, or canvas laundry baskets	Peterboro Basket Co., the Laundress, and Steele Canvas offer excellent options.
Plastic bathroom bins and caddies	Metal, wire, or canvas baskets	Your bathroom will instantly look better.
A plastic toilet brush and container	A wood-handled brush and metal container	For ideas, go to page 91.
Plastic document bins	Cardboard, wooden, or metal document bins	See "The Remodelista Storage 75" (pages 167–169) for sources.
Plastic wastebaskets	Metal, wooden, canvas, or woven wastebaskets	Buckets also work well.

What to Do with Excess Stuff: A Guide to Donating, Recycling, Selling, Swapping, and More

The things we live with need to earn their keep, and a big part of staying organized is regularly assessing what stays and what goes (and for the latter, what gets donated, sold, recycled, or tossed). Make this easy by setting up centrally located bins for gathering donations. Here's a guide to getting all your unwanted items out the door.

Donate

Be part of the reuse chain. Get rid of castoffs fast—and help nonprofits in the process—by donating instead of selling or tossing. If you have enough stuff, many organizations will make pickups. Be sure to get a donation receipt for your tax return.

CLOTHES

In addition to general-collection nonprofits like Goodwill (goodwill.org), try these three resources.

Dress for Success
dressforsuccess.org
Donate your work-appropriate clothing to help people entering the job force.

Planet Aid
planetaid.org
This nonprofit will resell your clothing and donate the profits to sustainable development projects in poor communities around the world.

Schoola
schoola.com
Launched by a school principal, Schoola resells clothing to help kids in need.

CONSTRUCTION MATERIALS AND LARGE APPLIANCES

Spare the landfill.

Habitat for Humanity's ReStores

habitat.org/restores

At these locally operated retailers, you'll find both new and gently used building materials as well as furniture, appliances, and home accessories. Sales from the stores benefit the house-building program.

Salvage Stores

Search for local options, such as BigReuse in New York City (bigreuse.org) and Urban Ore in Berkeley, California (urbanore.com).

CRAFT AND DIY SUPPLIES

There's always a demand for art supplies, fabric scraps, ribbon, floor tiles, CD cases—anything someone can use creatively.

Creative Reuse Stores

Search locally for organizations like Scrap in San Francisco (scrap-sf.org) and ReCreative in Seattle (seattlerecreative.org).

Schools and Educational Outreach Programs

Search locally for teachers' guilds or nonprofits that engage in educational outreach programs.

GENERAL HOUSEHOLD GOODS

Arc

thearc.org

A nationwide charity, Arc benefits people with disabilities.

Craigslist

craigslist.org

All Craigslist listings are free except for job offerings. So when you tire of searching for a buyer, list your goods as freebies and turn them over to someone who can use them.

Dog and Cat Rescues and Shelters

Search for local organizations. In addition to pet supplies, most often welcome used towels and bedding.

Donation Town

donationtown.org

This organization helps connect donors with local charities that make pickups.

FreeCycle

freecycle.org

FreeCycle is like Craigslist, but for free items only. Give and get on this site: in addition to posting offers for the taking, you can list things you're hoping to find.

Goodwill International

goodwill.org

Located all over the country, Goodwill is open to taking furniture and sporting equipment in addition to housewares.

Homeless Shelter Directory

homelessshelterdirectory.org

Look up shelters in your area and call to find out if what you've got matches their needs.

Salvation Army

salvationarmyusa.org

An international Christian charity founded in London's East End in 1865, the Salvation Army has become ubiquitous throughout the United States.

Web Thrift Store

webthriftstore.com

This charitable organization operates like eBay— sell your stuff and the proceeds go to the charity of your choice.

Sell

Selling used goods takes effort. If you're pressed for time, we recommend selling only high-ticket items and donating everything else.

ANYTHING

Craigslist
craigslist.org
This is our go-to method for selling locally; listings are free, but the burden of showing your wares and arranging a pickup or delivery is yours.

eBay
ebay.com
eBay takes a percentage of sales and can be confusing to navigate, but many sellers swear by it, not least for its international reach.

Nextdoor
nextdoor.com
This social network for U.S. neighborhoods is growing quickly; use it to sell your ladder to the guy up the street.

OfferUp
offerupnow.com
A tech-savvier version of Craigslist.

CLOTHES

Start with secondhand boutiques in a college town or indie neighborhood in a big city. Stores usually have posted buying hours and will pay you a percentage of what they sell your clothes for.

Poshmark
poshmark.com
Use the Poshmark cell phone app to post your upmarket labels in less than a minute.

The Real Real
therealreal.com
Offload your pricey jewelry, clothing, and accessories at this online consignment shop.

thredUP
thredup.com
thredUP welcomes the broadest array of clothing and accessories: any brand in any condition.

Tradesy
tradesy.com
Sell your gently used Céline sunglasses, Chanel bags, and other high-ticket items using this concierge service—they supply the shipping kit.

Vinted
vinted.com
Sellers set the price and keep 100 percent of sales on Vinted, which doesn't discriminate by brand.

FURNITURE AND HOUSEWARES

If you don't have the patience to hold a garage sale, consider one of these options.

Appliance Xchange
appliancexchange.com
Use this no-frills site to post free classifieds for your used appliances, and put your ten-year-old oven into the hands of someone who actually wants it.

AptDeco
aptdeco.com
List your vintage and contemporary furniture and housewares on this site for price-savvy shoppers.

Chairish
chairish.com
Chairish caters to the interior design set, so list your vintage offbeat wares here.

Everything but the House
ebth.com
The best way to sell an entire estate online, EBTH handles everything from pricing and photography to shipping and delivery.

Green Demolitions
greendemolitions.com
Green Demolitions—and its sister sites, Kitchen Trader (kitchentrader.com) and Renovation Angel (renovationangel.com)—will remove your entire kitchen or bath when you're ready to renovate and will sell, recycle, or donate each piece.

Previously Owned by a Gay Man
previouslyownedbyagayman.com
No, you don't have to be a gay man to sell furnishings at this online consignment shop.

Viyet
viyet.com
A high-end outlet for used designer furniture and accessories, Viyet takes a steeper commission than some—it starts at 50 percent—but its audience is seeking the best.

TECH GADGETS

It's easier than ever to sell your old devices—and keeping them in use is so much better for the planet than junking them.

Gazelle
gazelle.com
Sell your used mobile phones, tablets, and Apple products to Gazelle and they'll resell them online.

Gone
thegoneapp.com
Unload a broad array of electronics here, from headphones to cameras and smartwatches.

Recycle

For items too tattered or broken to be used again, do what you can to keep the materials in circulation.

Carpet Cycle
carpetcycle.com
Polyester carpet is one of the hardest things to dispose of, and it doesn't degrade naturally. Try this East Coast carpet recycler or search locally for one in your area.

Electronics Recycling
The EPA's recycling site (epa.gov/recycle) will point you to e-waste programs through which you can find an accredited recycler. It also lists big-box stores (such as Best Buy and Staples) that offer electronics recycling.

Mattress Recyclers
Check with your local jurisdiction to learn whether used mattresses can be resold or donated in your area. If not, search for a local mattress recycler.

Pay Someone to Take It Away

When all else fails, hire a removal service that will responsibly recycle the things they haul away.

1-800-Got-Junk

1800gotjunk.com

Pricey, but they'll take things (like moldy wall-to-wall carpeting) that no one else will touch.

Local Junk Removal Services

Search locally for these services—for example, Donation Nation in Washington, D.C., and Delete in San Francisco.

Avoid Buying in the First Place

Join the sharing economy: consider borrowing items you're unlikely to use very often (and that will take up precious storage space). Many public libraries lend far more than books (such as art, sewing machines, even fishing rods). And there's now a national network of tool libraries that loan things out for free or for a small fee. So instead of buying a tile cutter or a lawn mower, borrow one. Do an online search to find out what's available in your area. Also, go to Nextdoor .com and NeighborGoods.com to become part of a community of neighbors who are willing to share.

Our Favorite Sources for Storage Supplies

We advocate decluttering first, then sizing up your storage needs and using what you've got around the house before investing in anything new. That said, here are the sources we recommend for finding the problem-solving basics, from coat hangers to boxes to shelves. (For all stores with physical retail spaces, their locations are noted.)

Note: We choose thoughtfully designed products over mass-market disposable goods, and we like supporting small businesses and artisans. But we're also cost conscious: our sources are local as well as global, both specialty and mass market (several cater to the whole home and could appear in just about every category below—go to "Indie Design Shops" on page 204 and "National Stores" on page 208 to see these).

Baskets and Bins

All Hands
allhandsny.com
New York handbag designer Jen Stilwell spent three years working on boats in Alaska and beyond, which explains her affinity for canvas. Her bucket-shaped totes are modeled after traditional sailor bags with thick cotton rope handles.

Beckel Canvas Products
Portland, OR
beckelcanvas.com
From totes and duffels to tents, all products by this fifty-plus-year-old outdoors company are made of 20-ounce, marine-finished army duck canvas. We swear by Beckel's zippered "necessary bags." Most designs are stitched to order, and custom requests are an option.

Korbo
korbo.se
Initially geared to fishermen, Korbo's baskets are woven from single lengths of steel wire (no welding) and are not only rustproof but also indestructible. They come in a range of sizes, and several can be hung from their own purpose-built metal hooks. We use Korbo baskets all over the house.

The Laundress
New York, NY
thelaundress.com
Specialists in luxury laundry products, the Laundress teamed up with Beckel Canvas to create the Home Storage Collection, which includes hampers, totes, and storage bags.

Peterboro Basket Co.
Peterborough, NH
peterborobasket.com
The oldest basket-making factory in America, Peterboro weaves its baskets from flat strips of Appalachian ash harvested in New Hampshire, Maine, and Vermont. They're available in more than three hundred styles; standouts include an old-fashioned laundry basket with leather handles and nesting bushel baskets.

Rushmatters
rushmatters.co.uk
At Grange Farm in Bedfordshire, England, Felicity Irons is the keeper of an age-old English custom: she weaves trugs, baskets, bags, and floor mats of sturdy, fragrant bulrush. Spritz with water to rejuvenate.

Serax
serax.com
An Antwerp, Belgium–based company, Serax produces well-made domestic wares of all sorts. We especially love its line of Marie Michielssen–designed canvas baskets and bins that are gracefully proportioned and surprisingly sturdy.

Steele Canvas
steelecanvas.com
Steele of Boston has been making canvas industrial bins since 1921. And while initially intended for use on building sites, its hampers are now just as likely to be put to work in the laundry room, playroom, and garage.

Uashmama
shopuashmamausa.com
Pronounced "wash mama," this Italian line of baskets, bins, and other accessories is all made of a washable cellulose fiber (much like heavy-duty Tyvek). The results are a lightweight but resilient cousin to canvas.

Umbra
Toronto, Canada
umbra.com
Founded in 1979 by two childhood friends, Umbra is known for its clever solutions for all sorts of household challenges. We especially like Umbra's collapsible natural canvas Crunch Bin, available at the Container Store.

Verso Design
Helsinki, Finland
www.versodesign.fi/en
Based in Helsinki, Verso is run by Kirsikka Savonen and her two daughters, Tuttu Sillanpää and Tuuli Burman. The trio have their hand in a range of household products, including traditional Scandinavian baskets of pale birch and birch plywood storage boxes.

Beds with Built-In Drawers

Blu Dot

Locations worldwide

bludot.com

Blu Dot's Modu-licious bed collection consists of six steel drawers (available in a variety of colors) that run on the long side of a sleek wooden bed frame.

Crate & Barrel

Locations throughout the United States and Canada

crateandbarrel.com

Storage beds are a staple among Crate & Barrel's modernist offerings.

Duc Duc

New York, NY

ducducnyc.com

Visit Duc Duc for smart-looking (but costly) kids' beds with built-in drawers, bunk beds included.

Ikea

Locations worldwide

ikea.com

Designed with an eye to small-space living challenges, Ikea's ever-changing inventory always includes clean-lined and affordable beds with storage.

Muji

Locations worldwide

muji.com/us

These well-made, minimalist designs from Japan include beds with under-drawers and shelves.

Room & Board

Locations nationwide

roomandboard.com

Modern bed frames with add-on storage or trundles are a strong suit of the Minneapolis-based chain.

Urban Green

Brooklyn, NY

urbangreen.com

The Brooklyn workshop makes sustainable solid wood furniture using locally sourced materials. Urban Green's simple, made-to-order captain's beds are great space savers.

West Elm

Locations throughout the United States and Canada

westelm.com

West Elm's bed department caters to trend-conscious urban dwellers in need of storage.

Boxes

The Container Store

Locations nationwide

containerstore.com

We're long-standing fans of the Swedish company Bigso's extensive line of recycled fiberboard boxes, a Container Store staple made for the home office but useful all over.

Ikea

Locations worldwide

ikea.com

Ikea carries a changing assortment of boxes in solid colors and graphic patterns; we also like their cardboard box drawer organizers.

Carts

American Surplus Inc.
Rumford, RI
americansurplus.com
Based in Rhode Island—where it has a
530,000-square-foot facility—ASI is an online
clearinghouse for used industrial equipment,
including carts and gym lockers.

Everyday Design
everydaydesign.fi
This Helsinki workshop artfully blends aesthetics
with utility. Storage is Everyday Design's focus,
and its metal trolleys with birch wheels are
especially notable.

Ikea
Locations worldwide
ikea.com
Ikea applies its signature Scandi aesthetic to
every space challenge in the home. Its shelves
and carts, available in a range of styles and
finishes, are hard to beat for the price.

Kaymet
Kaymet.co.uk
Back in 1947, Sydney Schreiber set out to find
new uses for machinery that his Bermondsey,
England, business used to fabricate radar
equipment during World War II. Since then, his
London company, Kaymet, has specialized in
making anodized aluminum trolleys and trays that
are state of the art.

Urban Remains
Chicago, IL
urbanremainschicago.com
This architectural salvage gallery has an
impressive supply of vintage machine shop and
hospital carts, many of which have been stripped
down to their cold-rolled steel.

Closet Organizers

Bed Bath & Beyond
Locations nationwide
bedbathandbeyond.com
You have to separate the wheat from a lot of
chaff at Bed Bath & Beyond, but the chain is a
one-stop shop for home (and dorm) accessories,
from metal towel ladders to adjustable closet
organizing systems.

The Butler's Closet
thebutlerscloset.com
Barbara Harman founded the Butler's Closet
after she couldn't find conservation-quality drop
cloths for her upholstered furniture. Her line now
also includes 100 percent cotton, chemical-free
garment covers as well as shoe bags and English
horn clothes brushes.

The Container Store
Locations nationwide
containerstore.com
The Container Store offers solutions for all over
the house. We like their wooden coat hangers,
canvas shelf liners, and cardboard storage
boxes. Another highlight: Elfa modular metal
systems that enable you to create your own
storage-loaded closet.

Normann Copenhagen
Copenhagen, Denmark
normann-copenhagen.com
From washtubs to rocking sofas, this Danish
company offers contemporary Scandinavian
designs for the entire house. Its Toj Clothes Rack
(see page 114) is one of the nicest and best-made
options we've come across.

Clothes Drying Racks

The Columbus Washboard Company
Logan, OH
columbuswashboard.com
Laundry specialists since 1895, Columbus Washboard sells a small collection of what it calls "vintage laundry," including the Sheila Maid Clothes Airer, a classic British space-saving tool for drying linens and clothing. With the help of a rope and pulley, the rack is propelled to the ceiling, where warm air gathers and laundry is promptly dried.

Rejuvenation
Locations nationwide
rejuvenation.com
Started in 1975 as an architectural salvage shop, Rejuvenation now offers upgrades for all over the home and is part of the Williams-Sonoma brand. We like its Amish clothes drying rack (but be warned—assembly is required) and its basket and bins department.

Home Office Supplies

Design Ideas
designideas.net
The Container Store's source for metal mesh drawer inserts, enameled steel paper sorters, and more, Design Ideas also sells its affordably priced metal storage supplies on its own site.

Goods for the Study
New York, NY
goodsforthestudy.mcnallyjacksonstore.com
An offshoot of SoHo bookstore McNally Jackson, Goods for the Study is devoted to selling choice desks and all the accessories that go into and on top of them, lighting included. Many of the offerings are made in Sweden, France, and Italy.

Most Modest
mostmodest.com
A San Francisco start-up, Most Modest cloaks tech props in presentable packaging: see their Niko wooden power strip on page 133.

Present and Correct
London, England
presentandcorrect.com
P & C stocks an inspired assemblage of vintage-style stationery supplies, including wooden desk organizers, brass pen pots, and all manner of metal clips; "things we have enjoyed since school" is how the graphic designer owners put it.

This Is Ground
thisisground.info
This LA brand designs leather accessories, such as a Tech Dopp Kit and Cord Taco, for organizing gadgets at home and on the go.

Hooks, Peg Rails, and Storage Racks

Nomess
nomess.dk
Founded in 2007 by Suzanne Potts, who was in search of "products designed for the single purpose of making everyday life easier," the Copenhagen company makes interesting storage items, such as the aluminum So-Hooked Wall Rack fitted with movable aluminum S hooks.

Peg and Rail
Highland, MI
pegandrailusa.com
This family-owned Michigan outfit specializes in custom, reasonably priced peg rails (see pages 22–23).

Scout Regalia
scoutregalia.com
Los Angeles husband-and-wife team Benjamin Luddy and Makoto Mizutani specialize in playful utilitarian designs such as a powder-coated steel card table that hangs on the wall and doubles as a dry-erase board.

Stattmann Neue Moebel
stattmann-neuemoebel.com
This German fourth-generation family furniture-making business knows how to get the details right. The Marina Bautier entry hall unit featured on page 26 is a new Stattmann classic that comes in many configurations. Their wall-hung wooden shelving is also a favorite.

Indie Design Shops

ABC Carpet & Home
Delray Beach, FL, and Bronx and
New York, NY
abchome.com
What started out as New York's premier source for rugs has become an indoor souk offering everything from lighting to bedding, contemporary furniture, antiques, and a dazzling array of household accessories (including the Frisbee, a state-of-the-art French pedal-operated garbage can), all with an eco-friendly bent.

Amara
us.amara.com
An English interior design business that snowballed into a full-scale online retailer, Amara offers a number of top housewares brands, such as Iittala and Hay.

Analogue Life
Nagoya, Japan
analoguelife.com
The MO behind this Remodelista favorite is to preserve traditional Japanese craft and make it newly relevant. We love its wooden dustpans and cypress clothing racks fashioned after kimono stands.

Ancient Industries
ancientindustries.com
Created by graphic designer and Remodelista contributing writer Megan Wilson, Ancient Industries is an inspired compendium of British and European housewares that have been made the same way for generations.

A+R Store
Los Angeles, CA
aplusrstore.com
A+R carries well-selected modernist designs for LA living and beyond—including shelving options from all over the globe.

Brook Farm General Store

brookfarmgeneralstore.com

A Brooklyn pioneer, Brook Farm (now online only) stocks lovely basics: Riess wooden and enamelware canisters in four sizes, French string bags, and Senegalese woven laundry hampers.

Canoe

Portland, OR

canoeonline.net

Canoe's meticulously edited range of items—matte black mixing bowls, canvas totes, walnut peg-system shelves—includes many that hail from Portland.

David Mellor

Derbyshire and London, England

davidmellordesign.com

While David Mellor is synonymous with genius flatware design, the shop also carries a range of timeless household goods, such as plywood trays by David's son (and successor in the family business), Corin Mellor.

Everyday Needs

Auckland, New Zealand

www.everyday-needs.com

Founded by New Zealand stylist Katie Lockhart, this online shop specializing in "the pared-back, earthy, and honest" is a favorite source for inspired accessories, such as Japanese metal toolboxes and wooden doormats.

Father Rabbit

Auckland, New Zealand

fatherrabbit.com

Interior designer Claudia Zinzan's trove of simple and sublime housewares has something for every room.

Finnish Design Shop

finnishdesignshop.com

This comprehensive selection of Finnish and other Scandinavian products ranges from classics to designs by emerging talents.

Floyd

floyddetroit.com

This Detroit start-up aims to rethink apartment essentials. Floyd's platform bed and simple-to-install wall brackets are made to move with you.

The General Store

San Francisco and Venice, California

shop-generalstore.com

With its astute gathering of new and vintage wares, the General Store emphasizes California-made goods. Get your Beth Katz stoneware bowls and Luke Bartels live-edge cutting boards here.

Hive

hivemodern.com

This online shop is dedicated to modernism's greatest hits by Knoll, Herman Miller, and Alvar Aalto, among others.

Huset

huset-shop.com

Contemporary Scandinavian wares, from brightly patterned Swedish dishcloths to Verso baskets, are the focus here.

Kaufmann Mercantile

kaufmann-mercantile.com

Check out this online catalog for long-lasting and well-designed goods, complete with background histories.

Lekker

Boston, MA

lekkerhome.com

Lekker sources furniture and tableware with a Dutch and Scandinavian aesthetic. Storage options range from handcrafted wire and cane canisters to sculptural coatracks.

The Line

New York, NY, and Los Angeles, CA

theline.com

Set up as real homes, the Line's two stores are stocked with high-style versions of the stuff of life, all of it for sale. The goods are also available online and run the gamut from Michael Verheyden gray suede stools to Tenfold brass tissue box covers.

Lost & Found
Los Angeles, CA
lostandfoundshop.com

Five small storefronts collectively make up Lost & Found, owner Jamie Rosenthal's collection of housewares as well as fashion and art. A great source for woven baskets, ceramic trays, and wooden and jute stools that you won't see everywhere else.

Manufactum
Locations throughout Germany
manufactum.com

This trailblazing German department store is devoted to classic, no-nonsense designs for every inch of the house. Some standouts include enameled kitchen garbage cans, telescoping wooden sewing boxes, and wicker shopping trolleys. Manufactum's offerings run far and deep. And there isn't an off note in the bunch.

Merci
Paris, France
merci-merci.com

It's reason enough to make a trip to Paris: Merci's charmingly French collection of furniture, accessories, and office and garden supplies, including a good selection of enamelware trays. Profits (originally all and now some) go to education and development projects in Madagascar.

Mjölk
Toronto, Canada
mjolk.ca

Tastemaking young couple John and Juli Baker's boutique features Scandinavian and Japanese design (and often an inspired convergence of the two). In a world of modernist design stores, Mjölk stands out for its pure vision and can-do spirit.

Mûr
Winnipeg, Canada
murlifestyle.com

The carefully selected pickings from this small new online shop devoted to beautiful, "fully matured" everyday staples (*mûr* is French for "ripe") range from linen aprons to wood-handled scrub brushes, brass towel bars, and a great array of baskets.

Nalata Nalata
New York, NY
nalatanalata.com

An East Village gallery devoted to Japanese designs, Nalata Nalata has showcased specialty scissors made by a multigenerational family business, and the latest leather baskets and hooks from cult sneaker brand Hender Scheme. Find hinoki and copper bath buckets and stainless steel toilet paper trays in the online shop.

NK Shop
Los Angeles, CA
nickeykehoe.com

Interior design duo Todd Nickey and Amy Kehoe offer household accessories and European vintage finds with a boho-chic sensibility. For stylish storage, take a look at Nickey Kehoe's own line of powder-coated steel hanging hooks and wastebaskets.

Old Faithful Shop
Vancouver, Canada
oldfaithfulshop.com

A favorite resource for lighting and linens, Old Faithful also stocks tiered-wire produce baskets, stacking mugs, and other kitchen basics.

Pod
Cambridge, Massachusetts
shop-pod.com

This charmingly tiny housewares and clothing boutique is the American home base of Japanese line Fog Linen (shop-foglinen.com) and a good source for trays, linen dish towels, and our favorite Spanish wineglasses.

Schoolhouse Electric & Supply Co.
New York, NY, and Portland, OR
schoolhouse.com

Portland, Oregon–based lighting specialist Schoolhouse Electric now offers timeless, well-made designs for the whole house. See its storage and "domestic utility" departments for true-to-the-company's-name classroom-style steel wastebaskets, cafeteria trays, and wire gym baskets.

Sweet Bella
New York, NY
sweetbellausa.com
Sweet Bella is the exclusive U.S. distributor for a far-ranging group of finds, including the Ercol stacking chair, the Maison Martin Margiela champagne bucket, MT washi tape, and some of the best desk accessories on the planet. The company's boutique on New York's Lower East Side, Top Hat, is worth the pilgrimage.

Tiina the Store
Amagansett, NY
tiinathestore.com
This inspired collection of Scandinavian design classics came together when star fashion stylist Tiina Laakkonen was sourcing goods for her own home (see it in *Remodelista: A Manual for the Considered Home*).

Tortoise General Store
Venice, CA
tortoisegeneralstore.com
Visit Abbot Kinney Boulevard's hub of slow design from Japan for owner Taku Shinomoto's Hasami line of stackable ceramic plates, bowls, and mugs with wooden inserts that serve as trays and covers.

Trnk
New York, NY
trnk-nyc.com
Featuring handsome, Scandinavian-accented designs for the whole home, Trnk offers a wedding registry perfect for couples hoping to receive Normann Copenhagen steel pedal bins and Menu lidded oak bowls.

Kitchenware

Blisshaus
Oakland, CA
blisshaus.com
Wiebke Liu of Blisshaus is "on a mission to clean up the world, one kitchen at a time." Her focus is on the plastic-free pantry, and she is an advocate for buying in bulk, decanting, and cutting down on waste. Her business provides hands-on pantry organizing, and all of the key ingredients, such as airtight labeled glass jars, mesh produce bags, and flour sacks, are available in her online shop.

Flotsam + Fork
flotsamandfork.com
An under-the-radar kitchenware resource, Flotsam + Fork stocks a concise and delightful selection of practical storage accessories, many with a French accent.

Food52
food52.com/shop
This crowd-sourced cooking site is also a well-curated kitchen shop. Assembled with an eye to practicality and style, the goods at Food52 come from a wide range of sources, including small makers who provide the shop with exclusive versions of their designs.

March
San Francisco, CA
marchsf.com
Kitchenware as couture: in a carefully composed white-tiled boutique, March sells custom worktables arrayed with leather catchall boxes and market bags. March's spices come in chic black glass containers that keep the sun out.

Quitokeeto
quitokeeto.com
Food blogger and cookbook author Heidi Swanson is also a standout photographer and shopkeeper. Her online boutique is a favorite Remodelista source for inspired kitchen solutions, such as linen dish covers and magnetic knife racks of bleached maple.

Set & Co.
Dallas, TX
setandco.com

A sophisticated, Shaker-inspired housewares shop with an emphasis on the kitchen, Set & Co. stocks Sarah Kersten covered ceramic bowls, Italian cookware in bright colors, and an oak and leather Danish paper towel holder.

Sir/Madam
sirmadam.com

Inspired by flea market finds and a grandmother's cupboard, Sir/Madam's nostalgic designs include wooden spoons, heavy brass S hooks, and striped café au lait bowls.

Stovold & Pogue
theplaterack.co.uk

On their honeymoon in India, Jenny and Nick Stovold admired the space-saving stainless steel dish racks they spotted on kitchen walls. Back home in the UK, they founded their online shop, which imports the design in three sizes: mini, middle, and mighty.

Sur La Table
Locations nationwide
surlatable.com

Expect to find a far-ranging collection of kitchenware by top brands the world over. We turn to Sur La Table for well-priced and durable Duralex glass bistroware. (Tip: Duralex clear glass plates work well as see-through bowl covers for storing leftovers in the fridge.)

Whisk
Brooklyn and New York, NY
whisknyc.com

This mom-and-pop alternative to the big cookware chains sells well-made kitchenware and tabletop items, from metal canisters to Japanese lunch sacks.

Williams-Sonoma
Locations worldwide
williams-sonoma.com

While we rely on Williams-Sonoma mainly for classic tableware and serving pieces, their impressive range of kitchen storage solutions should not be overlooked. Weck jars, spice racks, and hammered copper canisters are a good place to start.

National Stores

Amazon
amazon.com

Amazon's reach is so far and wide that it often has what you're looking for—whether a natural moth deterrent, an Alvar Aalto bowl, or a Normann Copenhagen trolley—and can get it to you fast.

CB2
cb2.com

Crate & Barrel's younger sibling presents well-priced modernist basics, such as streamlined side tables (see the wall-hung version on page 105) and wire wall pockets (see page 31).

The Container Store
containerstore.com

The Container Store has developed an entire emporium devoted to organized living. Apply a discriminating eye and you can find all sorts of good solutions, from Elfa's dazzling modular shelving (for garages, pantries, closets, backs of doors, and more) to Bigso's cardboard boxes and International Design's simple metal mesh compartments for drawers.

Crate & Barrel
crateandbarrel.com
Founded in Chicago in the 1960s to introduce no-nonsense European design to America, Crate & Barrel holds true to its origins. Especially noteworthy: its Marimekko bedding, towels, and plywood trays (which can often be found on sale).

Design Within Reach
dwr.com
DWR jump-started the midcentury revival and turned many forgotten greats into bestselling designers. In terms of storage, credenzas and modular shelving are the chain's strong suit.

Ikea
ikea.com
Ikea has cornered Scandinavian household design for the masses, from streamlined desks (with built-in cord management) to metal pot lid holders. Though the inventory frequently changes, the chain continues to offer its most popular storage staples: Ekby wooden brackets and shelves and Grundtal kitchen rails, which start at less than twenty dollars.

Muji
muji.com/us
Celebrated for its simple, logo-free approach, Muji applies a succinct touch to every corner of the house. Among the notables: white dinnerware, lab-like glass canisters, bentwood trays, and covered porcelain food containers, all priced only a few notches above Ikea's.

Rejuvenation
rejuvenation.com
Rejuvenation has expanded from reproduction lighting to a focus on well-designed household nuts and bolts, storage included. It offers a good selection of baskets, from ash with leather handles to Korbo's woven steel designs.

Restoration Hardware
restorationhardware.com
Despite its origins, Restoration Hardware has veered away from hardware and conquered the whole house (contemporary art included). But search deep and you'll discover that the brand still offers classic, well-made metal hooks, cabinet pulls, mailboxes, and bookshelves, as well as an array of those handy overhead bathroom shelves known as train racks.

Room & Board
roomandboard.com
This Minneapolis-based purveyor features safe-bet modernist household design, including storage beds. We swear by their Spike Multiple Wall Hook, a reinterpretation of the Shaker peg rail in brightly colored powder-coated steel. And its basic cord management sleeves are better looking than most.

West Elm
westelm.com
Expect to find contemporary design channeled in rapid response to the latest trends. The brand is a reliable source for side tables, trays, woven baskets and bins, and wire mesh organizers.

Pegboards

Block
blockdesign.co.uk
Made in England, these wooden pegboards come in three sizes—the mini can stand on a tabletop—and a range of colors.

Dare To
daretodesignshop.com
A small Norwegian design studio, Dare To makes wooden pegboards, plus cubbies and shelves.

I Love Handles
Portland, OR
ilovehandles.com
This multifaceted design studio is home to the
SmorgasBoard, a magnetic wooden bulletin
board with movable pegs, hooks, shelves, and
pen boxes.

Kreisdesign
kreisdesign.com
Nikki Kreis's signature made-in-England
birch plywood pegboards are an elegant
reinterpretation of the storage classic.
See one of her designs in a home office
on page 125.

Uline
uline.com
Supplier of a huge range of industrial materials,
Uline is a good source for workbench-style metal
pegboards.

Shelving and Storage Systems

Atlas Industries
atlaseast.com
Atlas's finely crafted modular shelving comes
in solid wood and steel in a multitude of
configurations.

Design Within Reach
Locations nationwide
dwr.com
Midcentury storage to go with your Eames
lounge and Saarinen table—our favorite is Poul
Cadovius's adaptable Royal System Shelving
with a built-in desk. DWR also offers an array of
modular stackable drawers and cubes that can
be lifesavers.

Metro
metro.com
Metro's steel wire shelving systems on wheels
were originally designed for restaurant kitchens
and supply rooms—and are still popular in
commercial settings. But they're also a long-
standing favorite for home settings and are now
available from the Container Store.

Rakks
rakks.com
Favored by architects and widely used in
university settings, the straightforward, well-
engineered Rakks system has a no-nonsense
appeal that makes it equally at home in a
basement or a living room. You can add on to the
modular design, and owners tend to take it with
them when they move.

Vitsoe
vitsoe.com
The Mercedes of shelving, this infinitely flexible
shelving designed by Dieter Rams is a museum-
quality modern classic.

Stylish Utility

Best Made Co.
New York, NY
bestmadeco.com
What started as artist Peter Buchanan-Smith's collection of colorful axes has expanded to offer all sorts of artisanal gear for outdoors and in. If you want a handsome metal toolbox, leather zip case, or two-toned canvas bucket, Best Made will likely have what you're looking for.

Dover Street Market
Locations worldwide
doverstreetmarket.com
Rei Kawakubo's four-location wonderland is geared to the fashion obsessed (and the hungry—Rose Café has lovely outposts in the London and New York locations). It also features a tiny but worthwhile housewares department of utilitarian Japanese pieces, such as glass labware and enamelware trays, curated by the Good Design Store (gds.g-mark.org) of Tokyo.

Hand-Eye Supply
Portland, OR
handeyesupply.com
"Cool things you can use to make other things" is Hand-Eye's motto. That includes the supply store's own black canvas and denim aprons, Japanese enameled-steel toolboxes, and a selection of canvas tool bags, pouches, and leather-bottomed buckets.

Labour and Wait
London, England (two locations)
labourandwait.co.uk
This is our go-to source for well-made, timeless household essentials, including our favorite toilet brush and holder, enamelware jugs, and buckets of all sorts.

Objects of Use
Oxford, England
objectsofuse.com
Devoted to "international archetypes of everyday objects," Objects of Use stocks Swedish multiarm towel dryers, Japanese knives, and an international trove of brooms, brushes, and dustpans.

Yamazaki
www.theyamazaki.com
Look here for low-cost, space-saving storage solutions in metal and wood from a century-old Japanese brand (that started with ironing boards). Yamazaki sells its goods in the United States via Amazon and Wayfair. We swear by its slide-on door hooks, paper towel dispensers, and tool caddy.

Used, Vintage, and Antique

AptDeco
aptdeco.com
This New York City–based site makes it easy for urban dwellers to unload their furnishings—and to refurnish affordably.

Chairish
chairish.com
Chairish offers a platform for design fans to buy and sell "pre-loved decor." Vendors are based all over the United States, and goods are prescreened. You can shop by location and category, including room, style, and a section dedicated to storage.

eBay
ebay.com

Yes, it's still possible to get deals on the world's biggest auction site. Our tips? Shop locally (so that you can pick up bulky purchases and avoid shipping costs) *and* use advanced searches to shop internationally (source a design from the country where it was made and you'll likely pay less if it can be shipped reasonably).

Etsy
etsy.com

A site representing all manner of small purveyors, Etsy began as a digital storefront for crafters but now also hosts scores of vintage dealers. Sellers are based around the world, but shipping is generally reasonable. For those who like searching for needles in haystacks, Etsy is a great resource.

Everything but the House
ebth.com

A pioneer of the online estate sale, EBTH hosts hundreds of monthly sales across the country and, true to its name, auctions everything, often at bargain prices: bidding starts at one dollar, and there are no reserves. Find a sale near you to preview the goods firsthand. Warning: addictive.

1st Dibs
1stdibs.com

An umbrella site representing top antiques dealers of every specialty from around the world, 1st Dibs has also recently started representing leading contemporary designers and makers around the world.

Los Angeles Modern Auctions
Los Angeles, CA
lamodern.com

LAMA hosts three major auctions per year, featuring well-curated sales of twentieth-century art and design, and also stages exhibits. Founder Peter Loughrey is a font of midcentury design knowledge.

Previously Owned by a Gay Man
previouslyownedbyagayman.com

This nationwide online consignment shop sells a lot of showroom samples as well as used, vintage, and antique furnishings.

Viyet
viyet.com

Geared to global nomads, New York–based Viyet stands ready to help you sell your top-of-the-line sofa, rugs, and lighting when you move.

Wright
Chicago, IL
wright20.com

A combination auction house and online marketplace (click on WrightNow on their site for the latter), Wright specializes in modernist furnishings. Browse the storage section for midcentury shelving and nightstands by Paul McCobb, Jens Risom, and many others.

Unexpected Finds from Specialty Suppliers

For a lot of staples, we head straight to the trade stores: retailers that cater to makers and builders of all sorts, from artists to sailors to chefs. All sell no-fuss goods that are made to last. And all are easily accessible online (they also have brick-and-mortar stores worth getting lost in). Here's where we look and what we zero in on.

WHAT TO BUY AT

Art Supply Stores

- Art journals (to fill with pasted clippings of recipes and design inspirations)

- Boxes of all sorts, including flat files for artwork and photos

- Canvas work aprons

- Clipboards

- Dusting brushes

- Easels (for displaying paintings)

- Enamelware palette trays (for use as household trays)

- Glass paint jars (for storing dried herbs and spices)

- Map tacks and aluminum and wooden pushpins (nicer than the ubiquitous plastic)

- Masking tape and removable washi tape in colors and patterns

- Pencil cases

3 Sources to Consider

1 Blick (dickblick.com)

2 Jerry's Artarama (jerrysartarama.com)

3 Utrecht (utrecht.com)

WHAT TO BUY AT
Hardware and Building Supply Stores

- **Burlap** (as tablecloths and planter covers)

- **Canning jars** (for storing dry goods of all sorts)

- **Clothespins**

- **Cork bottle stoppers** (for sealing, among other things, spice bottles)

- **Drop cloths** (for use as tablecloths, no-stitch chair and sofa slipcovers, window shades, and more)

- **Empty metal paint cans** (as canisters for storing supplies, such as paintbrushes)

- **Galvanized steel buckets and wastebaskets**

- **Glass bottles**

- **Hang tags** (for labeling bins, baskets, and keys)

- **Kraft paper in rolls** (for use as paper tablecloths, shelf liner, and gift wrap)

- **Metal dustpans**

- **Rope, string, and twine**

- **Wire baskets**

- **Wooden and metal drawer organizers**

- **Wooden dish racks**

- **Wood-handled industrial brooms, brushes, and sweepers**

**3 Sources
to Consider**

1 Ace (acehardware.com)

2 Kilian Hardware Co. (kilianhardware.com)

3 Lehman's (lehmans.com)

WHAT TO BUY AT
Marine Supply Stores

- **Boat cleats** (for use as wall hooks and window shade catches)

- **Canvas totes**

- **Ditty bags** (for use as bathroom storage)

- **Gear hammocks** (for storing stuffed animals, bath toys, and more)

- **Metal dock ladders** (for accessing loft beds and hard-to-reach areas)

- **Recessed steel cabinet latches and other door hardware** (for a streamlined look)

- **Rope**

- **Stainless steel toolboxes** (for rust-free storage)

- **Teak captain's and deck chairs** (for foldable seating)

- **Teak cockpit tables** (for fold-out dining and work surfaces)

- **Teak kitchen wall racks** (for storing plates and glasses in one compact unit)

- **Under-the-shelf stemware holders** (for holding wineglasses upside down and making use of unused space)

- **Wire clips** (for closing food bags, hanging wet clothes to dry, and many more uses)

**3 Sources
to Consider**

1 Defender
(defender.com)

2 Jamestown Distributors
(jamestowndistributors
.com)

3 West Marine
(westmarine.com)

WHAT TO BUY AT

Restaurant Supply Stores

- Butcher block chopping boards

- Enamelware teapots and bowls

- Knives

- Modular steel shelving

- Pro refrigerators with glass doors

- Restaurant-weight dishware

- **Sheet pans** (as bases for dish drying racks and boot trays)

- Stainless steel cutlery sorters and knife holders

- Stainless steel dish drying racks

- Stainless steel mixing bowls

- Steel and wooden drawer dividers

- Steel pot racks

- Tea canisters

- **Tiffins** and other glass and steel food storage containers

- **Trays and fold-up bases** (for making portable tray tables)

- Wicker baskets

- Wood-handled scrub brushes

**3 Sources
to Consider**

1 Big Tray (bigtray.com)

2 Restaurant Supply (restaurantsupply.com)

3 Webstaurant Store (webstaurantstore.com)

WHAT TO BUY AT
Scientific/Labware Supply Stores

- Covered porcelain bowls

- Glass and porcelain funnels

- **Glass jars** (for storing dried herbs and spices, as well as small office supplies, such as tacks)

- Glass measuring beakers

- **Glass petri dishes** (for storing accessories, such as jewelry)

- **Metal instrument trays** (as all-purpose trays)

- Porcelain bowls with pouring spouts

- Porcelain mortar and pestles

- **Standing glass test tubes** (for use as vases; also for storing spices with cork stoppers from the hardware store)

**3 Sources
to Consider**

1 Karter Scientific (kartersci.com)

2 The Lab Depot, Inc. (labdepotinc.com)

3 Pyrex (pyrex.com)

Featured Architects and Designers

We are grateful to the following professionals who contributed designs featured in the book. For our complete listing of recommended architects and designers around the world, see the Remodelista Architect/Designer Directory at Remodelista.com.

Amanda Pays
Los Angeles, CA
amandapays.com
Amanda Pays

Elizabeth Roberts Architecture & Design, PC
Brooklyn, NY
elizabethroberts.com
Elizabeth Roberts

FRAMe
Orleans, MA
fram-e.com
Sheila Bonnell

Lindon Schultz
Los Angeles, CA
212-438-0677
Lindon Schultz

Michaela Scherrer Interior Design
Pasadena, CA
michaelascherrer.com
Michaela Scherrer

Oliver Freundlich Design
New York, NY
oliverfreundlich.com
Oliver Freundlich

Plain English
Suffolk, England
plainenglishdesign.co.uk
Katie Fontana

Rebecca Robertson Interiors
New York, NY
rebeccarobertsoninteriors.com
Rebecca Robertson
Marco Pasanella

Rees Roberts + Partners
New York, NY
reesroberts.com
Lucien Rees Roberts

Selldorf Architects
New York, NY
selldorf.com
Annabelle Selldorf

Solveig Fernlund
New York, NY
solveigfernlund.com
Solveig Fernlund

Steven Harris Architects
New York, NY
stevenharrisarchitects.com
Steven Harris

Acknowledgments

Many people contributed ideas and supported us on this project, including members of the Remodelista team: Francesca Connolly, Josh Groves, Janet Hall, Justine Hand, Christine Chang Hanway, Alexa Hotz, Sarah Lonsdale, Jessica Marshall, Annie Quigley, Michelle Slatalla, and Meredith Swinehart. And furniture designer Martin Forster assisted with construction.

A big thank-you to the following for allowing us to feature their homes in the book: Sheila Bonnell, Ann DeSaussure Davidson and Scott Davidson, Julia von Eichel and Alex Vlack, Howard Garrett and Philip Truelove, Alastair Hendy, Bianca and James Jebbia, Christina Kim, Michelle McKenna, Amanda Pays and Corbin Bernsen, Michaela Scherrer, Rebecca Scott and Jerome Ranawake, and Linling Tao.

And, most important, this book would never have come to be were it not for the talented crew at Artisan, including publisher Lia Ronnen, editor extraordinaire Bridget Monroe Itkin, creative director Michelle Ishay-Cohen, design manager Jane Treuhaft, senior production editor Sibylle Kazeroid, production director Nancy Murray, and assistant production and design manager Hanh Le. We ourselves are much more organized thanks to the experience.

In these pages, we sourced products from the following designers and retailers: ABC Carpet & Home; Ace Hotel; Aesop; Aesthetic Movement; All Hands; Ambatalia; Anchor Hocking; Ancient Industries; Beckel Canvas Products; Bed Bath & Beyond; Best Made Co.; Blick; Block Design; Brook Farm General Store; Bulthaup; Bürstenhaus Redecker; the Butler's Closet; By Laasen; Canvas Home; CB2; Christopher Specce; the Container Store; Crate & Barrel; David Mellor; Delphonics; Design Ideas; Dover Street Market; Flos; Fog Linen; Goods for the Study; Goose Barnacle; Hay; Hender Scheme; Home Stories; Ikea; Iris Hantverk; John Derian Company; Kinto; Korbo; Kreisdesign; Labour and Wait; the Laundress; Makié; Manufactum; March; Margaret Howell; Most Modest; M+A NYC; Muji; Mûr; Museum of Useful Things; Muuto; Nalata Nalata; Normann Copenhagen; Original BTC; Peg and Rail; Pottery Barn; Quitokeeto; Rejuvenation; Riess; Room & Board; Schoolhouse Electric & Supply Co.; Scout Regalia; Serax; Sir/Madam; Snow Peak; Stanley Ruiz; Stattmann Neue Moebel; Steele Canvas; Stovold & Pogue; Stutterheim; Sweet Bella USA; Top Hat; This Is Ground; Tomoko Azumi; TRNK; Uashmama; Umbra; Urban Green; Urban Outfitters; Urbansize; Verso Design; Victorinox; Williams-Sonoma; Wms & Co.; and Yamazaki.

Index